CAMBRIDGE LIBRARY COLLECTION

Books of enduring scholarly value

Cambridge

The city of Cambridge received its royal charter in 1201, having already been home to Britons, Romans and Anglo-Saxons for many centuries. Cambridge University was founded soon afterwards and celebrates its octocentenary in 2009. This series explores the history and influence of Cambridge as a centre of science, learning, and discovery, its contributions to national and global politics and culture, and its inevitable controversies and scandals.

The Western Manuscripts of Emmanuel College

M. R. James (1862-1936) is probably best remembered as a writer of chilling ghost stories, but he was an outstanding scholar of medieval literature and palaeography, who served both as Provost of King's College, Cambridge, and as Director of the Fitzwilliam Museum, and many of his stories reflect his academic background. His detailed descriptive catalogues of manuscripts owned by colleges, cathedrals and museums are still of value to scholars today. James's catalogue of the manuscript holdings of Emmanuel College was first published in 1904. Now reissued, it will be welcomed by librarians and researchers alike.

T0370833

Cambridge University Press has long been a pioneer in the reissuing of out-of-print titles from its own backlist, producing digital reprints of books that are still sought after by scholars and students but could not be reprinted economically using traditional technology. The Cambridge Library Collection extends this activity to a wider range of books which are still of importance to researchers and professionals, either for the source material they contain, or as landmarks in the history of their academic discipline.

Drawing from the world-renowned collections in the Cambridge University Library, and guided by the advice of experts in each subject area, Cambridge University Press is using state-of-the-art scanning machines in its own Printing House to capture the content of each book selected for inclusion. The files are processed to give a consistently clear, crisp image, and the books finished to the high quality standard for which the Press is recognised around the world. The latest print-on-demand technology ensures that the books will remain available indefinitely, and that orders for single or multiple copies can quickly be supplied.

The Cambridge Library Collection will bring back to life books of enduring scholarly value across a wide range of disciplines in the humanities and social sciences and in science and technology.

The Western Manuscripts of Emmanuel College

A Descriptive Catalogue

EDITED BY MONTAGUE RHODES JAMES

CAMBRIDGE
UNIVERSITY PRESS

CAMBRIDGE UNIVERSITY PRESS

Cambridge New York Melbourne Madrid Cape Town Singapore São Paolo Delhi

Published in the United States of America by Cambridge University Press, New York

www.cambridge.org
Information on this title: www.cambridge.org/9781108003087

This edition first published 1904
This digitally printed version 2009

ISBN 978-1-108-00308-7

THE

WESTERN MANUSCRIPTS

IN THE LIBRARY OF

EMMANUEL COLLEGE

London: C. J. CLAY AND SONS,
CAMBRIDGE UNIVERSITY PRESS WAREHOUSE,
AVE MARIA LANE.

Glasgow: 50, WELLINGTON STREET.

Leipzig: F. A. BROCKHAUS.
New York: THE MACMILLAN COMPANY.
Bombay and Calcutta: MACMILLAN AND CO., Ltd.

THE

WESTERN MANUSCRIPTS

IN THE LIBRARY OF

EMMANUEL COLLEGE

A DESCRIPTIVE CATALOGUE

BY

MONTAGUE RHODES JAMES, Litt.D., F.B.A.

FELLOW OF KING'S COLLEGE
DIRECTOR OF THE FITZWILLIAM MUSEUM

CAMBRIDGE:
AT THE UNIVERSITY PRESS
1904

𝕮𝖆𝖒𝖇𝖗𝖎𝖉𝖌𝖊:

PRINTED BY J. AND C. F. CLAY,
AT THE UNIVERSITY PRESS.

CONTENTS.

PREFACE.

THERE seem to be only two printed catalogues of the collection of manuscripts at Emmanuel College. The first is to be found in Thomas James's *Ecloga Oxonio-Cantabrigiensis* (London, 1600: p. 136). This enumerates nine volumes. The second is in the *Catalogi manuscriptorum Angliae* of 1697, and contains 137 articles, the first nine being those catalogued by Thomas James: nineteen others (nos. 49–67), in oriental languages, are not included in the present volume. This list was furnished to the Editors of the Oxford *Catalogi* by Joshua Barnes, and the last six items were gifts of his own to the College: to these he subsequently added many more, the bulk of them being works of his own composition. In H. Schenkl's *Bibliotheca Patrum Latinorum Britannica* (1901), II. 2 (nos. 2883–2914), is some account of the patristic manuscripts.

The collection is of very considerable interest. In Greek books it is unusually strong: the copy of the Pauline Epistles (no. 110), the *Hippiatrica* (no. 251), the Psalter (no. 253), and the Herodotus (no. 30) are all of a certain celebrity, and some of the fragments in no. 236 merit attention.

There is some excellent illuminated work in the Moralia of Gregory (no. 112), in a Bible (no. 116), and in nos. 106 and 252. Among the later texts, the volume of documents on the Council of Basel (no. 142) ought probably to be carefully examined by a specialist: the legend of St Aldate in no. 27 is at least a rare piece, and some of the poems in no. 106 are probably interesting. The Letters of the Martyrs in nos. 260–262 are perhaps sufficiently well-known.

The principal benefactors have been Thomas Leigh, B.D. (cir. 1667), who gave twenty volumes, Archbishop Sancroft, and Joshua Barnes. I do not know whether I ought to add William Bennett, Bishop of Cloyne, to the list: his gifts were numerous, but the greater part of them are notes of his own lectures.

A fair number of the manuscripts are interesting in respect of provenance. Barlings Abbey, Caen, Chichester, Faversham, Holmcultram, Kirkham, Norwich, Pershore, Selby, and Sheen all contribute. The volume from Caen (no. 29) is interesting as showing what I venture to call the Lanfrancian script, which took such firm root at Christ Church, Canterbury. Most of the Chichester books have good specimens of the cathedral press-mark.

A good many volumes noted in older catalogues (printed and manuscript) are not now to be found. A list of these is appended to this Preface along with the usual tables of corresponding numbers, and lists of donors and provenances.

In conclusion I must express the hope that I may have succeeded in justifying the confidence of the College, who have permitted me to contribute what I could to the elucidation of their ancestral possessions.

I hope, too, that my work may help to clear a path for the researcher of the future; if it conduces, indirectly, alike to the preservation of good old books and to the production of good new ones, it will fulfil all the expectations I have formed for it.

M. R. JAMES.

Tables showing the correspondence between the Numbers of the Manuscripts in Catalogi Manuscriptorum Angliae and those in the Present Catalogue.

I.

CAT. MSS. ANGL.	PRESENT NUMBER	CAT. MSS. ANGL.	PRESENT NUMBER	CAT. MSS. ANGL.	PRESENT NUMBER
1	9	37	2	95, 96	missing
2	21	38	20	97	103
3	110	39	70	98	missing
4	238	40	74	99 ⎫	260
5	37	41	40	100 ⎬	261
6	113	42	126	101 ⎭	262
7	38	43	116	102	34
8 (=80)	59	44	118	103	245
9	missing	45	114	104	31
10	246	46	printed	105	33
11	60	47	printed	106	250
12	69	48	125	107	? 255, 256
13	251	49–67	oriental	108–111	missing
14	241	68	112	112	247
15	4	69	264	113–116	missing
16	143	70	? 23	117	26
17	8	71	?	118	142
18	3	72	? 67	119	58
19	19	73	51	120	35
20	121	74	85	121	248
21	? 87	75	76	122	41
22	22	76	missing	123	120
23	? 24	77	94	124	84
24	? 81	78	91	125	missing
25	? 82	79	83	126	65
26	? 144	80 (=8)	59	127	27
27	5, 6, 7	81	86	128	98
28	39	82	62	129	missing
29	66	83	54	130	50
30	10, 11	84	16	131	35
31	242	85	29	132	61
32	253	86	73	133	117
33	239	87	56, 57	134	75
34	? 92	88	25	135	181 (v)
35	18	89–93	missing	136, 137	missing
36	17	94	28		

TABLE II.

PRESENT NUMBER	CAT. MSS. ANGL.	PRESENT NUMBER	CAT. MSS. ANGL.	PRESENT NUMBER	CAT. MSS. ANGL.
1	vac.	56, 57	87	114	45
2	37	58	119	115	—
3	18	59	8, 80	116	43
4	15	60	11	117	133
5-7	27	61	132	118	44
8	17	62	82	119	—
9	1	63, 64	—	120	123
10, 11	30	65	126	121	20
12-15	—	66	29	122-124	—
16	84	67	? 72	125	48
17	36	68	—	126	42
18	35	69	12	127-141	—
19	19	70	39	142	118
20	38	71	—	143	116
21	2	72	—	144	? 26
22	22	73	86	145-180	—
23	? 70	74	40	181 (art. v)	135
24	? 23	75	134	182-209	—
25	88	76	75	210-227 (oriental)	49-67
26	117	77-80	—	228-237	—
27	127	81	? 24	238	4
28	94	82	? 25	239	33
29	85	83	79	240	—
30	105	84	124	241	14
31	104	85	74	242	31
32	—	86	81	243, 244	—
33	131	87	? 21	245	103
34	102	88-90	—	246	10
35	120	91	78	247	112
36	—	92	? 34	248	121
37	5	93	—	249	—
38	7	94	77	250	106
39	28	95-97	—	251	13
40	41	98	128	252	—
41	122	99-102	—	253	32
42-49	—	103	97	254	—
50	130	104-109	—	255, 256	? 107
51	73	110	3	257-259	—
52, 53	—	111	—	260-262	99-101
54	83	112	68	263	—
55	—	113	6	264	69

List of Monastic and Other Ancient Owners of Manuscripts.

LIST OF DONORS OF MANUSCRIPTS.

LIST OF MANUSCRIPTS NOW MISSING.

1. From the manuscript Catalogue no. 257 : see p. 158.

76. Cancellaria et Praesidentia in Camera stellata, being 2 discourses in English upon yᵉ Court of Chancery and Star-Chamber, chartac. modern (=Cat. MSS. Angl. 76).

103. [Membranaceus.] 1. Malmsburiensis de dictis et factis memorabilibus Philosophorum : imperf. in initio. Non apparet hoc opus inter edita aut inedita huius Authoris, quorum Catalogum videre possis apud Balaeum et Pitsium.

2. Cassiodori ⎫
3. Capri ⎪ Orthographia. Collectore Guill. Malmsburyensi prout
4. Agroetii ⎬ ipse in fine testatur.
5. Albrici vel Alcuini¹ ⎪
6. Bedae ⎭

7. Censorinus de Die Natali, desunt 3 cap. in initio, ultimum in fine.
8. Apuleii de secta Platonica, Libri 11. imperf. in initio.
9. „ de Deo Socratis, a fine imperf.
10. „ de Physiognomia ab initio imperf. Non comparet inter op. edita.
11. Marbodii Brytanni, Evanx cognominat: liber Lapidum seu Lapidarius, Poema continens 60 capita cum Commentar : flor. author sub Edvardo Confessore postea Episcopus Redonens : apud Brytannos, quo fugit grassante apud nos Danorum tyrannide. Obiit Aᵒ. Sal. 1050, vid. Bale centen. 2, pag. 154 Scriptor. Brytann. et Pits de Illustr. angl. script. pag. 185.
12. Prisciani Philosophi lib. de iis in quibus dubitavit Chosroes I Magnus, Rex Persarum. seu solutiones Physicorum de quibus dub: Chosr: R. Pers. floruit A.D. 550, vid. Tab. Tallent.
13. Chronica Eusebii in latinam linguam ab Hieronymo translat.
14. Historia Troianorum imperf. a fine.
15. Physicon proteron.
16. Albericus vel Albricius de radiis Dictaminum. quis sit nisi ille Albricius Londinensis, qui floruit Aᵒ 1217 quamvis hic tractatus non inter eiusdem opera recensetur a Balaeo aut Pitsio viderint alii.
17. Joann. Sarisburiensis de septem septenis libellus a fine mutilat. neque hoc opus ei ascribitur inter opera recensita a Balaeo vel Pitsio. flor. 1182 Henr. 2ᵒ regnante.
18. Imperfecta quaedam super Apocalypsin.
19. De Praesagiis Tempestatum.
20. S. Hieronymus contra Helvidium de Perpetua Virginitate B. Mariae.

¹ Erat magister Caroli Magni Eboraco natus prout testatur Malmsburiensis.

105. A strange Acc^t of ye Temptation of Mr Robt Brigge, who thro X^t obtained ye Victory A^o 1574.

106. Commentarium in Summam Tho: Aquinat: item in Aristotelis Logic: Ethic: Physic: Metaphysic: Volumina 27 in quarto et 2 in octavo, qui aliquando Authorum nomina habent praefixa ordinis sc. Pontificii Scholasticos, Rev: Patr: Achillis Gagliardi Romae 1597: Jac. de Marmol :, Isaac: Hugonis, Doct: Westoni, Petri Wandenweile etc. omnes chartacei et moderni. [A few of these remain : see for instance nos. 255, 256.]

2. *In. Cat. MSS. Angl.*

9. Jo. de Sacro Bosco de sphaera. Transcriptum exemplar quo nihil elegantius. =James 9.

89. D. Thomae Tractatus de Jure et Justitia. Chartac. male scriptus.

90. Eiusdem tract. alius. paulo melius exaratus.

91. Eiusdem summae Theolog. 3 vol. Chartac.

92. Item 2 vol.

93. Doctoris Weston tractatus in D. Thomam.

95. Liber de Generatione et Corruptione.

96. Codex Astronomicus pervetustus. Chart. mut. principio et fine.

98. Tractatus quidam Philosophici et Resolutiones quorundam casuum Nationis Angliae post Reformationem.

107. Aristotelis nonnulla Latine 3 vol.

108. Aristotelis Logicae Physicorum etc. Compendium Latine male et subitaneo more scriptum.

109. Aristotelis Dialecticae Compendium 5 capp. comprehensum, chart. Item de Praedicamentis et περὶ ἑρμηνείας, chart. 2 vol.

110. Comment. in 3 lib. Aristotelis de anima. Chart. 4to.

111. Jacobi del Marmol. Soc. Jesu Hispalens. Comment. in 8 lib. Aristotelis Physicorum.

113. Marci Lyon Compendium Aristotelis simularum (*sic*). Chartac.

114. Controversia de Virtute Fidei per R. D. Jac. de Granada.

115. Eiusdem Explicatio de Justitiae originalis Natura, ubi de effectibus eius etc.

116. Eiusdem Generalis Controversia de Admirabili Eucharistiae Sacramento et Sacrificio ad undecim Quaestiones D. Thomae. 3 Partes viz. a Quaest. 73 ad 83.

125. Tractatus quidam nimis multi Philosophici, Physici, Ethici, Metaphysici, Lat. Chartac. male ut plurimum scripti et moderni in 4to.

Barnes's MSS.

136. Edvardi III Regis Angliae vita anglice transcripta e Codice C.C.C. apud Cantabrigienses.

137. Acta Filii Edvardi III Anglorum Regis exscripta e Codice C.C.C. apud Cantabr. Principium : Haec sunt acta bellicosa Illustrissimi Principis.

CORRIGENDA.

p. 18, l. 1, *for* Forsball *read* Forshall.

    l. 14, ,, English ,, England.

p. 57, l. 22, ,, qui *read* quis.

p. 67, l. 12, ,, Aspere *read* Aspice.

p. 87, l. 13, ,, ffeoffœtis *read* ffeoffatis.

p. 92, l. 32, ,, servunt *read* serrunt.

p. 109, l. 14, ,, Hatton ,, Halton.

p. 110, l. 19, ,, Suttlini ,, Suttliui.

p. 119, l. 15, ,, Bennet ,, Bennett (and so elsewhere).

p. 130, last line (note), *for* listed *read* noticed.

p. 139, l. 18, *add* perhaps meaning R. Spindleton.

p. 140, l. 4 from bottom, *for* Cent. xi *read* Cent. xv.

NOTE. The table of correspondences between Bernard's numbers and my own does not always agree with those given in the body of the book, for I have altered my views of the identifications in some cases since the descriptions were printed off.

CATALOGUE OF MANUSCRIPTS.

MSS. I. I. 1   ? vac.

1. VISITATION OF STAFFORDSHIRE.

Paper, 13½ × 9¼, ff. 63, and Index. Cent. xvi late, clearly written, and with arms neatly drawn.

The Visitation of Staffordshire by Robert Glover *alias* Somerset Herald, Marshall to Wᵐ Flower *alias* Norroy King of Arms 1583.

I. I. 2   C. M. A. 37

2. AUGUSTINI QUAEDAM.

Vellum, 13½ × 8¾, ff. 194 + 3, double columns of 57 lines. Cent. xiii late, very well written. Initials in blue and red. Probably English hand.   2 fo. illum creatarum.
The verso of the flyleaf has old pencil notes.
Collation: 1 flyleaf, 1¹²–14¹² 15⁸ | 16¹² 17⁶ : 2 flyleaves.

Contents :

1. Inc. prol. b. Augustini de mirabilibus ueteris et noui testamenti.
   (*P. L.* xxxv. 2149) . . . . f. 1
   Ueneratissimis urbium et monasteriorum episcopis et presbiteris
      —aliqua non fastideant.
   Capitula.
   Cum omnipotentis dei auxilio
      —exemplo huius castigarentur.
2. Augustinus contra Faustum. Aurelii Aug. doctoris contra
   Faustum manicheum liber inc. (XLII. 207) . . . 18
   Faustus quidam fuit genere affer.
      —et catholici esse possitis. Aur. Aug. c. Faustum
      manicheum expl. liber.

3. Inc. liber primus Aurelii Augustini contra aduersarium legis
    et prophetarum (XLII. 603) . . . . . . f. 94
    Librum quem misistis fratres.
    —quam tocius explicabo.   Aur. Aug. doct. c. adv. leg. et
    proph. lib. secundus expl.

4. Disputatio S. Aug. contra Felicianum hereticum quam postea
    scriptam filio suo tradidit. (XLII. 1157) . . . . 109 *b*
    Extorsisti mihi dilectissime fili
    —retribuere mercedem.   Ex(p)licit disp. S. Aug. c.
    Felic. heret.

5. Aur. Aug. de uera innocentia liber inc. (XLV. 1859) . . 114
    Innocencia uera est
    —si te ipsum respexeris.   Aur. Aug. de uera innoc. lib.
    expl.

6. Inc. liber S. Aug. de spiritu et littera. (XLIV. 199) . . 123
    Lectis opusculis que ad te
    —ipsi gloria in sec. sec. Amen.   Expl. lib. S. Aug. Ep.
    doctoris eximii de sp. et litt. ad marcellinum.

7. Inc. libellus B. Aug. ep.   De cognicione uere uite. (XL. 1005)   133 *b*
    Sapientia dei que os muti aperuit
    —corpus columbe condidit.   Expl. libell. B. Aug. Ep. de
    cogn. uere uite.

8. Inc. libellus a(d) Volusianum.   (Ep. 132) . . . . . 136 *b*
    Domino illustri
    —multum salutat.

9. Epistola Aug. ad Ytalicam.   (Ep. 92) 139
    Domine eximie
    —melior explicare.

10. Inc. liber b. Aug. de collatione x. preceptorum ad decem
    plagas. (XXXIX. 783) . . . . 139 *b*
    Non est sine causa
    —auxiliante d. n. I. C.   In sec. sec. Amen.

11. Inc. libellus b. Aug. ep. de uisitacione infirmorum. (XL. 1147)   140 *b*
    Uisitacionis gratia nepoti meo
    —qui uiuit per omnia sec. sec. Amen.   Expl. liber b.
    Aug. Ep. de uisit. infirm.
    f. 144 blank.

12. Inc. prol. Aur. Aug. de doctrina christiana. (XXXIV. 15) . 145
    Libros de doctrina (from the Retractations).
    Sunt precepta quaedam
    —facultate disserui.   Expl. lib. S. Aug. de doct. christ.

13. Hic inc. lib. b. Aug. Ep. ad inquisiciones Januarii. (Ep. 54) . 170 *b*
    Libri duo quorum est titulus.
    In primo ergo quod de manna dixi
    —lecturam atque daturam.
    Most of f. 176 *b* blank.

14. In a different hand of the same time:
    Aduocatio (? adnotatio) S. Aug. operum plurimorum . . 177

A list of books. De achademicis libri iii.

...

De mendacio lib. unus. Expl. capitula.
Inc. prefatio Aug. Ep. (the Retractationes). (XXXII. 583).
Iam diu istud cogito.
Ends f. 193 *a*: retractare cepissem.
On 194 *b* and flyleaves are pencil notes and one late note in ink.

I. 1. 3   C. M. A. 18

3. BEDAE HISTORIA.
GIRALDUS CAMBRENSIS.

Vellum, $14\frac{1}{2} \times 9\frac{3}{4}$, ff. 120, double columns of 46 lines. Cent. xv
(1481), well written with excellent ornaments.   2 fo. nec mora
On f. 1 : Jo. White, 1613.   *or* peruenisse.
Written for John Gunthorpe : see below.
Collation: $1^{10}-12^{10}$.

Contents :

Not mentioned in the Rolls Series edition, or in the Catalogue
of Materials by Hardy.

The ornament, which is in the form of borders and initials at the beginnings of the books, is very elaborate. The border (three sides) on f. 1 is partly on a gold ground, partly on blue and partly on white. It consists of a mixture of conventional and natural flowers, including roses and blue columbines. The other borders are of the same description. The style betrays, I think, a foreign, probably Flemish, artist.

The following badges and mottos occur.

1. f. 1 and elsewhere a lion's head erased *arg.* langued *gules*.
2. On f. 2. Motto. *Virtuti parent omnia*, also subsequently.
At the beginning of Lib. ii and in most of the subsequent borders a cannon *argent*.
At beginning of Lib. iii f. 31. Motto. *Mais pour le m(i)eulx.*
Lib. iv has no border.
Giraldus Dist. i f. 87. Initials J. G., and shield, party per pale. *Dexter*: quarterly.
1 and 4, *arg.* a chevron *gules* between three suns *sable* (probably *argent* turned black).
2 and 3, *gules* a chevron *sable* between three lions' heads erased *arg. Sinister.* Within a bordure *sa.* engrailed: *gules* a bend dexter *arg.* bearing three leopards' heads *or* on *azure*, between two lions' heads erased *arg.*

The shield occurs only here. The other devices are repeated. I believe them to be the arms, badges and initials of John Gunthorpe, Dean of Wells, a prominent book collector, who died in 1498. He built a portion of the Deanery at Wells and employed stone cannon (guns) in the decoration of the building, as a *rebus* on his name.

I. I. 4   C. M. A. 15

4. ASTRONOMICAL TABLES.

Paper, 13¾ × 8⅞, ff. 298 written: many blank leaves at each end. Cent. xvi or xvii early, very well written.

A large collection of Astronomical Tables. At the top corner of the first page is 1602 written small. This may quite well be the date of the book. I find no name.

Perhaps the greater part of the Tables are called

Tabulae Prosthapherisis.

I. 1. 5, 6, 7   C. M. A. 27

5, 6, 7. BIBLIA HEBRAICA.

Vellum, 15 × 9⅝, three volumes, double columns of 28 lines.
Cent. xii, xiii, finely written.
In the 2nd cover of vol. 1 is this notice:

> This very fine MSS. (so) of the Hebrew Bible was given to Emmanuel College Library
> by Dr William Bedell, Bp of Kilmore in Ireland, who had been educated in the College
> and had been many years Fellow of it. He took his degree of B.D. in the year 1599. Soon
> after this he was sent to Venice in quality of Chaplain to the English Ambassador (S^r
> Henry Wotton) at the time of the Interdict. During a stay of ⅜ years in this place,
> amongst many other improvements, he applied himself very closely to the study of the
> Hebrew, in which he made a great progress by the assistance of R. Leo the Chief
> Chaiham of the Synagogue there. It was by means of the Rabbi that he purchased
> this MSS. which is said to have cost him its weight in silver.
>
> It was very near being lost in the year 1641 when he was sent to Prison (where he
> soon after died) and his palace at Kilmore and all his papers and goods were seized by
> the Irish Rebels. But a grateful Irishman whom the Bp had sometime before converted
> from Popery went among his countrymen and brought out this MSS. and a few other
> books to him. See the Bp's Life by Dr Burnet.

There is a fine illuminated title on a separate pair of leaves,
prefixed to the first volume. It is certainly not by the hand
which has executed other decorative work in the body of the book,
and to my eye the colouring at least suggests a Western—I might
almost say an English—hand.

I. 1. 8   C. M. A. 17

8. ROB. DE BRIDLINGTON SUPER EPISTOLAS PAULI.

Vellum, 13⅞ × 8⅞, ff. 232, double columns of 42 lines.   Cent. xii,
fine hand.   2 fo. clementis.
Collation: 1⁸–29⁸.
On the flyleaf an erased title Jeronimus (?) super Epistolas (xv).

Contents:

> De epistola ad Romanos. Opening words of the chapters of the
>   Epistles .   .   .   . f. 1
> Inc. prol. compilationis in epistolas Pauli apostoli .   .   . 1
> Sicut et aliarum mearum compilationum.

Ends f. 1 *b*: et pro peccatis collectoris huius operis ROBERTI de
berlinctuna fideliter apud deum intercedat.
Prologues of Jerome, Mag. Lambertus etc. follow.
The text of the Epistles is in red, comment in black.
Ends imperfectly on Heb. xii (ut maneant ea que sunt immobilia):
declaratur celi et terre que.

Leland and Tanner call the author Robertus Scriba. He was
4th prior of Bridlington and flourished in 1180. Another MS. of
this Commentary (a copy of which Leland saw at Queens' College)
is in the University Library, Dd. 8. 14. It is not a common book.

I. 1. 9   C. M. A. 1
9. PROPOSITIONES ET TRACTATUS.

Vellum, 14¼ × 10⅜, ff. 247 + 1, double columns of 51 lines.
Cent. xv, xvi, in a somewhat current hand.
On the flyleaf a list of contents, and:

Orate pro anima Reu^{mi} patris domini Johannis Kemp nuper Episcopi S. Rufine
sacrosancte Ecclesie Romane Cardinalis Archiep. Cantuar. Et pro anima domini Thome
Kemp episcopi London. nepotis eiusdem domini Iohannis Kemp.

Collation: 1 flyleaf, 1⁸–16⁸ (wants 8) 17⁸–31⁸.

Contents:

1. Proposicio facta per Mag. Jo. de Gersono Cancellar. Parisiens.
    nomine Uniuersitatis coram Petro de Luna Benedicto 13mo . f. 1
    Benedic hereditati tue sanctissime pater Benedicte
       —et beato complemento in futuro per gloriam prestante
       eo qui est benedictus in sec. sec. Amen.
2. Tractatus eiusdem de pollutione nocturna et diurna . .   5
    Scripsi quidem aliqua super preparacione ad missam
       —deus faciens contemp^{ne} prouentum qui est benedictus
       in sec. Amen.
3. Tractatus editus per mag. Petrum de Alliaco sacre theologie
    professorem eximium postea uero Cardinalem Cameracensem
    contra fr. Joh. de Montesono de ordine predicatorum nomine
    uniuersitatis Parisiensis   9
    Apostolicis petri verbis edocti
       —super habundanciam expleuisse. Expl. iste tract. ad
       honorem dei et virginis gloriose.
4. Proposicio facta coram consistorio per mag. P. de Ailliaco
    contra mag. Joh. de Montesono . . . . .   36 *b*
    Veritatem meditabitur guttur meum.
       —propositum supposicionis preambule.

f. 40 *b* blank.

5. Inc. Francisci petrarche poete laureati Epistola super psalmos
    septem ad Sigramors de paueriis ex equite armate milicie
    nacionis picardie Cisterciensem monachum exhortatoria ad
    Religiosi principii perseueranciam in modum qui sequitur . f. 41
    Semper et unus uocibus tuis
    —Venetiis decimoquinto Kal. Apr. Amen. deo gracias.
        Expl. epistola.
    Inc. psalmi. Heu michi misero etc. Expl. meditaciones seu
    psalmi franc. petr.

6. Sequitur libellus super celebracione misse editus a mag. Jo. de
    Gersomio quondam can. eccl. paris.   43
    Dubitaui frequenter et diu
    —hoc est omnis homo. deo gracias. Expl. quidam trac-
    tatus plurimum utilis super celebracione misse quem
    composuit mag. Ioh. de gersomio cancellarius ecclesie
    parisiensis.

7. Sequitur de jurisdicione potestatis ecclesie seu de potestate pape   49 *b*
    Appostolus ad Romanos x^{mo} loquens de iudeis
    —alienum presidentem in tali loco.
    Expl. tract. de jurisdict. eccl. potest. siue de potest. pape, mag.
    Heruei Britonis ordinis predicatorum ut dicunt aliqui.

8. Reuocatio facta per fratrem (blank) saravium ord. pred. ex
    ordinacione facultatis theologie a.d. mill. quadring. vicesimo
    nono mense martii   76
    Ex vesperiis meis quidam fuerunt scandalizati.

9. Inc. tract. de potestate ecclesiastica et de origine iuris et legum
    per mag. Jo. de Gersono theol. doct. et eccl. paris. cancell.
    compilatus a.d. 1417 in concilio generali constantiensi   .   76 *b*
    Potestas ecclesiastica debet
    —vel de iure vel de facto.
    Colophon, practically repeats title, adding date : die sexta febr.
    Notes on plenitudo potestatis etc. .   .   .   .   .   88 *b*

10. Inc. quidam tract. quem composuit mag. Jo. de Gersomio doctor
    in theol. cancell. nostre domine paris. (de auferibilitate pape)   88 *b*
    Venient autem dies.

11. Tres questiones de ordine Jurisdictionum quibus populus regitur
    compilate per fr. Durandum ord. pred. episcopum meldensem   95
    Circa originem potestatum
    —pro ecclesia determinare uidetur. Expl. etc.

12. (In table). Tract. quidam de potestate papali et Regia viz.
    questio disputata utrum papa habeat dominium et iuris-
    dictionem tam in temporalibus quam in spiritualibus   .   101
    Rex pacificus Salomon cui dedit dominus diuicias
    —in quietem et tranquillitatem uitam agamus. Amen. Expl.

13. (In table). Tract. de iurisdictione imperii et auctoritate summi
    pontificis per fr. Alex. de Elpidio Augustinensem.
    Capitula .   .   .   .   109 *b*

Determinacio compendiosa etc. Quoniam apud multos uertitur
in dubium . . . . f. 110
—uel obuiare non potest qui est bened. in sec. sec. Amen.
Expl. libellus de potest. eccl. et iurisd. imperii editus a fr.
Alex. de S. Elfridio sacre pagine eximio professore ord.
heremitarum S. Aug.

14. Proposicio facta coram Rege Henrico vito et tribus statubus in
parliamento London. anno regnorum suorum decimo per
mag. Guill. Erardi sac. theol. doct. Ambaissiatorem ville
Parisiensis 123
Nescio Christianissime
—audiat terra uerba oris mei. f. 127 *b* blank.

15. Proposicio coram papa facta per mag. P. de Aylliaco contra fr.
Jo. de Montesono ord. fr. pred. 128
Pater sancte in nomine tuo serua eos.

16. Proposicio facta in consistorio per eundem contra eundem . 129 *b*
Veritatem meditabitur.

17. Alia eiusdem coram papa contra cancell. Paris. . . . 132
Domine uim patior.

18. Sermo eiusdem de S. Bernardo. Dedit ei cor ad precepta . 134

19.   „   de S. Ludouico. Vide reliquit egiptum . . 137

20.   „   in Sinodo ambianis. Sacerdotes tui induantur 139

21.   „   in Sinodo in eccl. Paris. Hoc iam queritur
inter dispensatores . . . . 141 *b*

22. Exemplar litterarum responsiuarum ex persona Vniuersitatis
Paris. ad epistolam tholosanam 144
Postulata in primis rex christianissime
Including Letter of Benedict to Charles of France, and reply.

23. Lectiones Joh. de Gersono de uita spirituali . . . 149 *b*
The 3ʳᵈ 4ᵗʰ 5ᵗʰ 6ᵗʰ precede the 1ˢᵗ which begins on f. 167 *b*.
Ego uos baptisaui aqua
and is followed by the 2ⁿᵈ, which ends f. 174 *b*.
Expl. 2ᵃ lectio. alias quatuor quere prius, scilicet terciam 25
folio priori et incipit pergere et sic consequenter ponuntur
4ᵃ 5ᵃ et 6ᵃ. mauricius folpe. This is the name of the scribe.
f. 175 blank.

24. Inc. liber dialogorum gerarchie subcelestis inter orthodoxum
catholicum et cathecuminum pantascium inquirentem de
reformacione ecclesie militantis 176
Quia actoris est intencio etc.
Cathecuminus primo loquitur dicens. Instancia mea quotidiana.
In 4 books: ending f. 205 *b*: et erit benedictus et gloriosus in
sec. sempiterna. Amen. Expl. 4ᵘˢ liber gerarchie subcelestis recollectus senis per quemdam de ordine predicatorum
cuius nomen utinam deleatur de libro uiuencium temporaliter
ut scribatur finaliter in libro uite.
Capitula follow. Another copy at Wolfenbüttel, Cod. Aug.
2834.

I. 1. 10, 11   C. M. A. 30

10, 11. HAYMO SUPER EPISTOLAS.

Vellum, I. $13\frac{1}{2} \times 9\frac{1}{2}$, ff. 94; II. $12\frac{3}{4} \times 9\frac{7}{8}$, ff. 182, double columns
of 41 lines. Cent. xii, in a fine bold hand. Upper parts of the
first 16 leaves of Vol. I. damaged and neatly replaced in cent. xv.

2 fo. passionem.

On f. 1, Tho. Leigh, and an old number 55.

Probably from Faversham Abbey. At the end of Vol. II. are
documents relating thereto.

Collation: I. 1^8–3^8 (wants 1) 4^8–6^8 (gap) 14^8 15^8 (wants 1) 16^8
(wants 2) 17 (two left) 7^8 8^8 (wants 8) 18^8.

II. 1^8–13^8 14^{10} (6 canc.) 15^8 (quire gone) 19^8–24^8 25^6
(wants 6). Occasional drawings on lower margin
of leaves.

Contents:

On 181 *b* is a deed of cent. xii, xiii.

Sciant tam presentes quam futuri quod Gilbertus de Wlecumbe et homines eius de Wlecumbe calumpniabantur quandam partem pasture in bosco Rogeri de kyngesnade hereditar' tenend'. Quam pasturam ecclesia S. saluatoris de ffauersham recuperauit liberam et quietam ab omni calumpnia iudicio cur' Reg' coram Justi(ciari)is Regis etc....Harum conuencionum isti sunt testes: Hamo de Truleg', Paganus de Campana, Ric. paysr', Geruasius de Osperng, Walt. tomtrinius, Radulfus de frendisberi, Clemens de assug', Eustachius nepos Gilberti, Rog. filius Galfr. de cnolle, Eadwynus de badenor' et Willelmus et conuentus de fauersham.

Then an inventory badly written late in cent. xv (1483).

Memorandum that y dan John Raby hath leueft yn the froytur and oostry thes nesessaryys att the feste of myhyllmas hee beyngge dyschargyd and yen the furste yere of kyngge Rycharde the III hys rayne. Item a maser callyd qwenes multys bolle. Item a grete maser callyd the prior dan john ffauersham ys maser and ther to ys a ffayyre prynte of the trynyte. Item a maser callyd the chynke bolle and ther yn ys a prynte in the bottom of dan wyllyam holland. Item a grete maser wᵗ a honycorne yn the bottom therof and ther to ys a grete couerkyll of maser bownde wᵗ a bond of syluyr and gyltte and a grette knoppe therouer syluyr and gyltte. Item a grette maser for wyne wᵗ a prynte yn the bottom ther of wᵗ a ffygure of owre lady and wrytynge abowte here aue marya. Item a smale brokyn maser wᵗ a prynte yn the bottom and Jhesus wrytyn ther yn. Item a lytyll prety maser wᵗ a pryntt yn the bottom and ther ys dauyth wᵗ hys harpe and ther to ys a prety couerkyll wᵗ a ffayre knoppe. Item a maser wᵗ a couerkyll and a knoppe of syluyr and gylte that master ffrogennall gaue. Item vi syluyr sponys. Item a grette boll pece of syluyr. Item a lytyll stondyng pece of syluyr. Item a tabyll clothe of dyapyr callyd qwene molltys cloth. Item a nodyr cloth callyd bylsyngton ys cloth. Item a nodyr dyapyr cloth callyd mastres thorneberys cloth. Item v curteynys for the v tabelys yn the froytur. Item v playnne tabyll clothys yn the froytur. Item a schortt towell of dyapur that margarite talbott gaue to the froytur. Item ii longe towellys of playne cloth. Item vij wypyng towellys for the cloystur. Item iiii saltsalers and on wᵗ a couerkyll. Item a newe presdent cloth. Item a grette spruce cheste wᵗ loke and kay. Item a nodyr grette cheste wᵗ owtte locke or kay and ii lytyll betyllys of boxe. Item a grette tancarde bownde w^t hyerryn a bowtte and ij gustetys.   Item vj platerrys and vj dyschys and v sawsserrys.   Item a maser callyd dan pers ys maser.   Item a yerryn grate for collys.   Item a baskett for to sett brede and iii crusys.   [Added.] Item anodyr dyapyr towell John pers and ij moo present clothys.   Item a lytyl maser w^t a skalop schell.

f. 182 *b.*   To the Oostry.

Item yn the grette chambur ii bede stedellys.   Item ii feddyrbeddys a grette bolstur. Item ij lytyll bolstres.   Item a grett couerlett for ye grete bedde w^t branchys and byrdys. Item a grett couerlett to the todir bedde wrowth full of Rosys.   Item vj payr of chetys. Item a cheste w^t locke and kay.   Item to the grett bedde a seller a tester and iii corteynys all of redde saye and a redde couerlett w^t owtt anny werke therreon.   Item to the todyr bedde a seler a tester and a curten all of blewe saye.   Item a copborde.   Item a table w^t ii trestellys.   Item ii formemys and a longe chayr.   Item in the lytyll chambyr a bedde stedyll.   Item a blewe couerlett w^t smale Rosys.   Item ii payr of blankettys. Item ii canstykys and on w^t ij nosys.   Item a mattres and ij pyllawys and ij old pyllawberrys and on new.

I. 1. 12, 13   vac.

12, 13. CHRYSOSTOMI HOMILIAE SUPER MATTHAEUM.

Vellum, 13⅞ × 10¼, ff. 337, double columns of 30 lines.   Cent. xi, xii, in a fine large hand.

Given by Dr Samuel Parr.   On the flyleaf is this note :

This MS. formerly belonged to the learned Adam Askew, M.D., and after his death came into the possession of his eldest son Adam Askew, by whom it was given to me in the year 1790, in testimony of his regard for me as his Schoolmaster at Stanmore, Middlesex, and as the intimate Friend of his deceased Father.

With sincere and great pleasure I present it to the Library of Emmanuel College, as a mark of my respect for the Master and Fellows of the Society in which I had the honour to be educated; and the Manuscript, I suppose, will be the more acceptable to them, as having once been the property of Dr Askew, and his Son, who were Members of the same College, and who, like myself, took a lively interest in its Prosperity and its Fame. Samuel Parr.

Halton Parsonage, Warwickshire, August 19th 1814.

There is also a reference to the Eton edition of Chrysostom.

Vide Editionem S. Chrysostomi Editionis Savilianae Etonae impressam anno MDCXII. Vol. 2, p. 4, l. 20 τῶν λεγομένων ἦσαν.
Hic codex continet ultimam partem primae Homiliae.
Homil. 2—15.

Pasted into the cover is a printed slip from F. Field's edition of the Homilies, Cambr. 1839, descriptive of the MS. (there termed B), and noting the *lacunae.* It was lent for nearly two years to the editor, who collated it throughout.

Collation: α⁸⁷ (wants 1–5) β⁸ γ⁸ δ⁸ ε⁸ (wants 1, last leaf now precedes 2nd) ϛ⁸–ιθ⁸ κ⁶ κα⁸–κγ⁸ κδ⁸–κϛ⁸ κζ⁶ κη⁸–λβ⁸ (5 canc.) λγ⁸–λζ⁸ (wants 6) λη⁸ (wants 1) λθ⁶ μ⁸–μδ⁸.

Contents:

Homiliae S. Joannis Chrysostomi in Matthaeum.
Beginning imperfectly in Hom. 1
   τῶν λεγομένων ἦσαν.
Vol. I. ends in Hom. 16
   ὑψηλὴ γένηται ἡ φλὸξ οὐχὶ ξύλων μόνον ἀλ-
Vol. II. continues
   -λὰ καὶ λίθων
and ends in Hom. 30 (35 Savile)
   μόνον εἰς ὄνομα μαθητοῦ ἀμὴν λέγω.
Savile ii. 241, l. 31.

Field's note on the contents runs as follows:

" Codicis quod reliquum est continet Homilias xxxv priores, exceptis xxv—xxix, quae nunquam in eo exstiterunt : nam Homilia tricesima numero xxv notatur. Praeterea temporis damno perierunt partes quae sequuntur. Ab initio operis ad p. 9 A, l. 1 : a p. 49 B, l. 1 ad p. 50 C, l. penult.: a p. 108 B, l. 5 ad ὅπερ p. 109 C, l. 5 : a p. 273 A, l. 6 ad τοῦτο p. 274 A, l. 3 : a p. 352 C, l. 3 ad p. 353 B, l. 5 : a πόσῳ p. 355 A, l. 5 ad p. 356 A, l. 1 : postremo omnia post p. 401 B, l. 8."

I. I. 14, 15   vac.

14, 15. CHRYSOSTOMI HOMILIAE SUPER MATTHAEUM.

Vellum, 14⅛ × 10¼, ff. 275, double columns of 33 lines. Cent. xi, finely written.

Given by Dr Samuel Parr.

Collated for Field's edition in which it is cited as M.

Collation: 1⁹ (two sheets = 4 leaves, and another leaf left) 2⁸ (wants 1) ε⁸ (wants 4, 5) ϛ⁸–ιε⁸ ιϛ⁴ (or 8 wants 3–6) ιζ⁸–κα⁸. ff. 144. κβ⁸–κη⁸ (wants 4, 5, 8) κθ⁸–λε⁸ (wants 2) λϛ⁸ (wants 4, 5) λζ⁸ λη⁸ (6 a fragment) λθ⁹ (one left). ff. 131.

Contents:

S. Joannis Chrysostomi Homiliae in Matthaeum.
Begins imperfectly in Hom. 48 Savile
   ἡ δὲ καὶ συγκατασκευάζει τὸ δρᾶμα (Sav. ii. p. 307, l. 36)
   to εἰκόνα θεοῦ γενόμενον τύπτης (p. 311, l. 34).
Then on f. 6 Hom. 49 Savile
   τὸ δρᾶμα αὐτοὺς ἐφόβησε (p. 313, l. 22).

Vol. I. ends in Hom. 68: οὐδὲ ὄναρ ταῦτα φαντασθῆναι δύναμαι
(p. 434, l. 20).

Vol. II. continues καὶ οὕτως ἐμπρησθεὶς
and goes on (with lacunae) to Hom. 90: ἰδία δὲ τὸ τοῦ ἀγγέλου
(p. 549, l. 44).

The last leaf contains Hom. 90, p. 550, l. 37, πυκτεύοντες to p. 551,
ll. 36, 37.

The last words are mutilated and indistinct.

The other lacunae are in Hom. 50, Savile, p. 321, l. 26 to 323, l. 10:
after f. 17.

After f. 102, Hom. 62, Savile, p. 395, l. 2 to 398, l. 25.

After f. 195, Hom. 76, Savile, p. 477, l. 23 to 479, l. 7.

After f. 197, Hom. 77, Savile, p. 400, l. 34 to 481, l. 27.

After f. 246, Hom. 84, Savile, p. 522, l. 35 to 523, l. 29.

After f. 255, Hom. 86, Savile, p. 531, l. 20 to 533, l. 8.

Most of the text of f. 272, Hom. 89, Savile, p. 547, l. 18 to 548, l. 12.
The writing hangs from lines ruled with a dry point.   The headings
(texts) of the Homilies are in very pretty semi-uncials, usually red.

I. 1. 16   C. M. A. 84

16. AUGUSTINUS DE VERBIS DOMINI.

Vellum, 11¾ × 8⅝, ff. 278, 33 lines to a page.   Cent. xii, in two
good hands resembling those of the Christ Church Canterbury MSS.
From Chichester Cathedral.   At top of f. 1 is:

Aug. de verbis   ℥. xiiij.
(domini) secundum Matheum.   ii^do fo. textus | finis seculi .

And at the bottom is the mark

℥. xiiij.

Collation: 1⁸–5⁸ (7 canc.) 6⁸–35⁸ (wants 8).

The first hand, which is very beautiful and delicate, changes to a
blacker and larger one on f. 40 (42) a, in the middle of the page.
Towards the end of the volume the lines become longer.   There
are a good many old pencil scribbles.   Initials in green and red.

Contents:

List of sermons, headed
Sermo S. Augustini de uerbis domini in euangelio secundum matheum   f.   1
Inc. sermo S. Aug. de uerbis euangelii sec. Matheum   .   .   3 b
Agite penitentiam appropinquabit enim regnum celorum.
Euangelium audiuimus et in eo dominum.

Sermo 65. de ueteribus scripturis etc. contra arrianos. Sancta et
diuina . . . . 189 *b*
Sermones (*66 to end*) de uerbis apostoli. Audiuimus ueracem
magistrum 192
Ends f. 278 *b* : ego erogem ueniet qui exigat. (*P. L.* xxxviii, xxxix.)

The MS. is tender from damp at each end.

I. 1. 17   C. M. A. 36

17. AUGUSTINUS DE TRINITATE.

Vellum, 12¼ × 8⅞, ff. 136, double columns of 36 lines. Cent. xii,
well written.   2 fo. cens non potui.
On f. 1. Tho. Leigh.
From Barlings Abbey. At the foot of col. 2 of f. 1 is:

Dominus Galfridus de Edenham canonicus ecclesie Lincoln. dedit abbati et conuentui
de Barlyng*es* istum librum.

Collation : 1⁸–6⁸ (8 canc.) 7⁸–15⁸ (7 canc.) 16⁸ 17⁸ 18².

Contents :

1. Inc. Capitula Augustini episcopi de Trinitate. (XLII. 819)   f.   1
    Sententia b. Augustini de libro retractationum . . . 1 *b*
    Epistola b. Augustini ad Aurelium 2
    Domino beatissimo.
    Inc. liber primus Aurelii Augustini de sancta Trinitate . 2
    De triplici causa erroris etc.
        Lecturus hec. Initial in gold.
    Other handsome initials, in blue and red for the most part, occur.
    Liber xv ends f. 136 *a* : ignosce et tui.
2. In another hand, rather of charter-type.
    Exemplar priuilegii indulti Regno Scotie 136
    Celestinus episcopus seruus seruorum dei karissimo in Christo
    filio Willelmo Regi Scotie.
    Cum uniuersi Christi iugo subiecti apud sedem apostolicam
    patrocinium inuenire debeant.
    Ends. Nulli ergo omnino hominum liceat hanc paginam nostre
    constitutionis et prohibitionis.
3. Innocentius ep. seruus etc. Karissimo in Christo filio Willelmo
    illustri Scott*ie* Regi eiusque successoribus salutem in
    perpetuum . . . . 136 *b*
    Cum uniuersi fideles
        —se nouerit incursurum. Dab. Lat(erani).

I. 1. 18   C. M. A. 35

18. TABLES.

Paper, oblong, 12 × 14½, ff. 25.   Cent. xvi, xvii.
On f. 1. Tho. Leigh.
A collection of Mathematical Tables, very well written.
Called in the old Catalogues

Sinus Logarithmicus.

Each page contains the calculations for one Degree..   They go
as far as 44 Degrees.

I. 1. 19   C. M. A. 19

19. BEDA SUPER PROVERBIA ETC.

Vellum, 13½ × 9¼, ff. 151, double columns of 40 lines. Cent. xii,
in a fine upright hand.   2 fo. ria eius.
On the flyleaf. Tho. Leigh.
Also, erased

liber de......sci petri ex dono......

At end, beginning of an indenture, xvi.   Joh. Smythe de wylbrm
(Wilbraham ?).
Collation : 1⁸–19⁸ (wants 8).

Contents :

Inc. expositio uen. Bede presb. de tabernaculo et uasis eius ac
uestibus sacerdotum.
Locuturi iuuante domino.
The hand changes at f. 121 to one of later (xiii) type.
Ends f. 151 a: quia isti sunt semen cui benedixit dominus.

I. I. 20   C. M. A. 38

20. WITELONIS PERSPECTIVA.

Vellum, 12⅜ × 8⅞, ff. 198, 46 lines to a page.   Cent. xiv, very
well written.   Good initials in red and blue.   2 fo. ut cum per.
At bottom of f. 1 :

Iste liber est de perquisito fr. Stephani Coulyng. ordinis predicatorum (erasure: post
cuius decessum pertinet communitati (or conuentui) fratrum eiusdem ordinis Tᵛruye)
precium iii marc. argenti puri et pertinet ad conuentum Tᵛruye (erased) post decessum
predicti fratris.

Below this is a still more carefully erased press-mark.
Collation : 1⁸–13⁸ 14⁶ 15⁸ 16¹⁰ 17⁶ 18⁸ (+a slip) 19⁸ (+slip)
20⁸–24⁸ 25¹⁰.
At the end on the lower margin :

perspectiua magʳⁱ Vitulonis, sunt xxv quaterni.

Contents :

Inc. perspectiua Mag. Witelonis Thuringorum et polonorum filii.
Continens 805 proposiciones.
Veritatis amatori fratri Wilhelmo de Morbeka Witelo filius Thuringorum et polonorum eterne lucis irrefracto mentis radio felicem
intuitum et intellectum perspicuum subscriptorum. Uniuersalium
encium studiosus amor.
The figures are drawn with great neatness on the margins. There
are many marginal annotations.
The work consists of ten books ending f. 198 b
nichil coeternum nichil eque bonum estimantes, cui sit honor et
gloria per infinita secula. Amen. Explicit enim hoc opus
gloriosissimum per quod omnes philosophi ad huius seculi per-
uenerunt gloriam et honorem. Beatus qui nouerit eius secreta.
Expl. perspectiua mag. Witelonis. Continet autem proposiciones 805.

Printed at Basle, 1572.   A fine MS. now at Oxford (Ashmole
424) was formerly at Peterhouse.

I. I. 21   C. M. A. 2

21. BIBLE IN ENGLISH.

Vellum, 14¾ × 10, ff. 350 + 2, double columns of 63 lines. Cent. xiv late, finely written.
On the flyleaf:

> John Wickleff's translation performed by him Anno Domini 1383.
> This copy will give forty pounds.

Modern binding: there has been a pattern on the fore-edges.
Collation: 1 flyleaf, 1⁶ 2⁸–44⁸, 1 flyleaf.
The headlines are in gold throughout, written on scrolls. The initials are in gold on a ground of pink and blue, with white pattern. Smaller initials in blue with red flourishing.

Contents:

> Here bigin(ne)þ (a) table wiþ a rule þat teechiþ in what book & chapitre of þe bible vne shal finde eueri l(ess)oun (*at masse* above line, later) pistil & gospel þat ben rad in þe chirche bigynnynge atte firste Sondai in aduent . . . . f.   1
> In four columns: names of Sundays, etc., and references in red: beginnings and endings of lessons, etc., in black.
> Proper of Time   1
> Commemoraciouns (Missae Votivae)   3
> Proper (and Common) of Saints   3
> Ends f. 6 *b*: and euere þanke we: oure lord eendeles in trinite.
> Genesis etc. without prologues, except in the cases specified .   7
> Full border in gold on pink and blue, with white pattern.
> The Prayer of Manasses forms c. xxxvii of 2 Paral.
> There is a short prologue on Job added in lower margin,
> > Joob was a very man in kinde.
> Notes on the occasions of the Psalms are added in the margin in the earlier part of the Psalter.
> There is a prologue to the prophets,
> > As seint ierom seiþ in þe prolog of isaye
> and one to Baruch.
> There are prologues to the books of the New Testament.
> The Epistle to the Laodiceans does not occur.
> The Apocalypse ends f. 350 *b*,
> > here endiþ þe bible
> > Jhesu helpe us for we ben feble.
> There are a few explanations of old words (xvii) on the flyleaf.

In the edition of Forsball and Madden it is quoted under the symbol P.

It is no. 118 in their List of MSS. (I. lvi).

They assign it to about 1420. It gives the later Wycliffite version. "The text and orthography agree very remarkably with the Arundel MS. 104."

I. 2. 1   C. M. A. 22

22. BIBLIA.

Vellum, 9⅝ × 6⅜, ff. 470, double columns of 51 lines. Cent. xiii, in a very good hand.   2 fo. tam non posse.

Has suffered from damp.

At bottom of f. 1, in large letters (xiii, xiv),

> Biblia ex dono Johannis de Smi^{ton}.

The only parish in English which seems possible is Smeaton in Yorkshire.

Collation: 1^{14} 2^{14} 3^{12}–6^{12} 7^{16}–13^{16} (one canc.) 14^{16} 15^{16} 16^{8} 17^{16} 18^{16} $19^{?}$ (ten left: gap after 5) 20^{12} 21^{16} 22^{16} 23^{10} 24^{16} 25^{16} (one canc.) 26^{16} (one canc.) 27^{16} 28^{16} (three canc.) 29^{12}–34^{12}.

On f. 83 is (xvi)

> Thomas Everingham is my name a childe of onest.

Everingham is in Yorkshire.

Contents :

> Jerome's Prologues.
> Genesis—2 Paralipomenon. Prayer of Manasses follows without a break.
> Ezra, Nehemiah. Apocrifa neemie (= 3 Esdr.).
> Tobit—Job.
> Psalter. Gallican.
> Proverbs—Ecclus.
> Isaiah—Malachi.
> 1, 2 Macc. There are illuminated (not pictured) initials to the prologues and text of 1 Macc.
> Evv. Paul. Epp. Acts. Cath. Epp.
> Ending imperfectly in James ii. 12.

I. 2. 2   ? C. M. A. 70

23. BIBLIA.

Vellum, $9\frac{1}{4} \times 6\frac{3}{8}$, ff. 358, double columns of 53 lines.   Cent. xiii, in a good small hand.   2 fo. hucusque.
Given by Mag. Foxcroft huius olim Collegii alumnus et scholaris discipulus, Ecclesiae nunc Gothamensis Rector.
At the end (xv) Biblia M. Willelmi erased.
On the flyleaf (xv)

Prec. v. marc. Et si contingat quod librarie communi vendetur volo quod habeat infra summam suprascriptam pro vi*s*. viii*d*. ut causam deprecandi valeat habere pro anima nuper possidentis.

Collation: 1 flyleaf, 1^{16}–11^{16} 12^{14} 13^{16}–15^{16} 16^{24} 17^{16}–19^{16} 20^{14} 21^{14} 22^{20}.
On f. 1 the name Thompson (?) erased.

Contents :

Prologues of Jerome.
Genesis—2 Par. Prayer of Manasseh follows without a break.
1 Esdras (Ezra, Neh.), 2 Esdras (1 Esdr. of Apocr.).
Tobit—Job. Gallican Psalter.
Prov.—Ecclus., Isa.—Malachi, 1, 2 Macc.
Evv., Paul. Epp. (Colossians occur twice, the second time after
  2 Thess.), Acts, Cath. Epp., Apoc.
Interpretationes nominum (Aaz—Zuzim).
Memorial verses on the books.
Note from Greg. *Moralia* XXXI.
Unfinished list of books and chapters.

The illuminated initials are in good style, not historiated.

I. 2. 3   ? C. M. A. 23

24. BIBLIA.

Vellum, $8\frac{1}{2} \times 5\frac{5}{8}$, ff. 509, double columns of 53 lines.   Cent. xiii, very well written.   2 fo. cum legeret.
Collation: 1^4 2^{16} (wants 1) 3^{16}–23^{16} (16 canc.) 24^{16}–30^{16} 31^6 (6 canc.)
32^{16} 33^{18} 34^4.

Contents :

Prologues of Jerome.
Genesis (wanting f. 1)—2 Paral.   Prayer of Manasseh follows
  without a break.
Ezra, Neh., 2 Esdr. (1 Esdras of Apocr.), Tob., Judith, Esth., Job.

Psalter (Gallican).
Prov.—Ecclus.
Isa.—Malachi, 1, 2 Macc.
Evv., Paul. Epp., Acts, Cath. Epp., Apoc.
Interpretationes nominum: Aaz—Zuzim.
At the end : precium biblie istius xj marc'.
There is a complete set of prologues.

The following historiated initials in very good ordinary style
occur : they are abnormally small, except the first.

Prol. Jerome (monk) writing at desk. Dragon, dog and hare in border.
(*Genesis* gone.) *Exod.* Moses and two Jews. *Lev.* Three Jews sacrifice. *Num.*
Moses puts Tables of Law in Ark. *Deut.* Moses receives the Law.
Jos. God in sky addresses Jews. *Jud.* Warrior kills a man (head downwards).
Ruth. None.
1 *Reg.* One man beheads another. 2 *Reg.* David (?) rends his clothes. Saul (?) dead
on *R.* 3 *Reg.* David in bed: Abishag and courtier. 4 *Reg.* Ahaziah falls headlong to
R. from tower.
1 *Par.* Creation of Adam. 2 *Par.* Solomon throned, with sword.
1 *Esdr.* Builders. Cyrus below. *Neh.* gives cup to king. 2 *Esdr.* Jew sprinkling
altar.
Tobias reclining : bird above. *Judith* beheads Holofernes in bed. *Esther.* Ahasue-
rus reaches down his sceptre to Esther. Haman hangs below.
Job on his dunghill: wife on *R.*
Beatus vir. David with harp. *Dominus illuminatio.* David points to his eye.
Christ above. *Dixi custodiam.* Similar. *Dixit insipiens.* Fool with club and cake.
Salvum. Christ above, David below: half-lengths. *Exultate.* David plays on 3 bells
with hammers. *Cantate.* Clerks singing at lectern. *Dixit Dominus.* Trinity: Father,
Son and Dove.
Prov. Solomon with rod. Rehoboam on *R.* *Eccl.* Solomon holds up flower and
speaks to a man on *R.* *Cant.* Virgin crowned and child. *Sap.* Solomon with sword.
Warrior on *R.*
Ecclus. The Church, with cross and chalice.
Isaiah sawn in sunder by two men. *Jeremiah* stoned. *Lam.* Jeremiah. City on *R.*
Baruch. Monk writing. *Ezekiel* in bed: heads of the four beasts above. *Daniel* in
den caresses lion: half-lengths. *Hosea* speaks to Gomer. *Joel* addresses two men.
Amos keeping sheep. Christ's head in sky. *Obadiah* takes bread (?) to prophet in
tower on *R.* *Jonah* emerges from fish: city above. *Micah* addressed by God in sky.
Nahum. Falling city on *R.* *Habakkuk.* Like Micah. *Zephaniah* with axe
smites golden idol. *Haggai.* Single figure. *Zechariah.* Similar. Christ's head above.
Malachi. Like Micah.
1 *Macc.* Warrior with sword. Christ on *R.* 2 *Macc.* Jew gives letter to messenger.
Matt. Jesse tree, with figures of David (?), Virgin, and Christ. *Mark* with book.
Luke writing. *John.* Like Mark.
Romans. Paul with sword. 1 *Cor.—Philem.* Similar. *Heb.* Paul addresses Jews.
Acts. Group of four figures (Ascension or Pentecost).
James. None. 1, 2 *Pet.* Peter with key. 1, 2, 3 *John, Jude.* Single figures.
Apoc. John writing, surrounded by church towers.

I. 2. 4   C. M. A. 88

25. HIERONYMUS CONTRA RUFFINUM.

Vellum, 9⅜ × 6⅛, ff. 104, 33 lines to a page.   Cent. xii early, in
an excellent hand.
From Chichester.   At bottom of f. 1 is

Jeronimus contra Ruffinum Seffridi Episcopi ij^{do} fo. | *magistrum* | fj. xxv.

Collation : i⁸–xiii⁸.

Contents :

(See *P. L.* XXI. 541, XXIII. 397.)

I. 2. 5   C. M. A. 117

26. Hieronymus contra Iovinianum, etc.

Vellum, 10 × 6⅞, ff. 102, 29 lines to a page.   Cent. xii early, in
a good hand.

From Chichester.   On bottom of f. 1 is

Jeronimus contra Jouinianum cum aliis ij^{do} fo. | *quanquam* | ꝟ. xxiiij.

Collation: 1⁸–7⁸ (8 canc.) 8¹² (wants 12) 9⁸–12⁸ 13⁴.

Contents:

I. 2. 6   C. M. A. 127

27. Miscellanea.

Vellum, 9¾ × 6⅝, ff. 244 + 1, single and double columns.   A
number of tracts bound together, mostly of cent. xiii.

Probably from Chichester.   In a kalendar at the end the
dedication of Sompting Church occurs.   Salisbury documents also
occur.

Collation: 1 flyleaf. I. 1¹². II. 2⁸ 3¹²–15¹² 16¹⁰. III. 17⁸–22⁸
(wants 8) 23⁸ (wants 1) 24⁴. Quire 1 is numbered in an old hand
from 238 to 249.

Contents :

On the recto of the flyleaf is a record connected with Salisbury. The *R.* portion is gone. In ecclesia Cath. Sarum sunt altaria infra scripta videlicet. Summum altare in choro. Item in vestiario .1. altare b. marie virginis. Item in capella beate m..../ Item in parte boriali capelle b. marie .1. altare S. Johannis Euangeliste. Item in parte austr..../ unum altare S. Stephani. Item ex opposito borial. hostium chori .1. altare s. marie.../ sancte katerine. Item ex oposito austral. hostium chori .1. altare s. marie magdalene et vin (?).../ Item iuxta hostium occidental. chori viz. in parte borial. chori 1 altare S. Thome martiris.../ regis et martiris cum xi. m. virg. adiuncta. Item 1 altare S. Edmundi confessoris. Item 1 altare S. Johannis.../ omnium reliquiarum ad inuicem. Item iuxta hostium occidental. in parte austral. 1 altare b. marie.../ b. laurencii et Vincencii. Item 1 altare b. Michaelis. Item in coro ecclesie coram magna cruce in parte borial..../ Item in parte australi 1 altare S. Andree apostoli. Item in solar' coram crucifixo coram altari......

Nomina Regum in ecclesia Sarum.

	Le Roy Henry frere au roy William Rous.
	Le Roy Stiepne.
In sinistra	Le Roy Henri counte de Angewe.
manu interioris	Le Roy Henri Jun'.
chori Sarum.	Le Roy Richard.
	Le Roy Johan.
	Le Roy Henri med.
	Le Roy Edgar.
	Le Roy Edward de Shaftbury.
	Le Roy Ethelred.
In dextra	Le Roy Edward de loundres.
parte int.	Le Roy Harold.
chori Sarum.	Le Roy William conquerour.
	Le Roy William Rous.
	Le Roy Edward le primer.
	Le Roy Edward le secounde.
	Le Roy Edward le III^{ce}.
(In au)strali	Le Roy Richard de Burdeux.
(parte) chori	Le Reyne Anne sa femme.
Sarum.	Le Reyne Elyzabeth sa femme.

1. A quire in late xiiith cent. hand of sermons; f. 245 originally blank has had some matter written in it in cent. xv, viz. Consideranda in confessione secundum mag. Robertum S. Victoris Parisiensis.

De Antichristo. Antichristus de tribu dan ignobilis in obscuro loco babilonie nascetur etc.

2. Hic. inc. allegorie b. Gregorii (really by Petrus Comestor: see II. 1. 20) . . . . f. 1
In precedentibus premissa descripcione originis.
Ends imperfectly in lib. iii.
f. 9, miscellaneous matter, partly in another hand, including a poem.
Sacerdotes mementote / Nichil maius sacerdote / Qui ditatus sacra dote / Ruga caret omnis note. Ending: Corpus Christi quod prophane / Manus tractant ille mane.

3. Short legends on the Festivals 10
Festiuitates sanctorum apostolorum seu martirum.
On f. 12 b two long sections De S. Egwino, f. 19 S. Elphege, 22 b Mildred, 23 a Kenelm, 24 Sampson, 26 b Frideswide.
Ends with a story of Fulbert of Chartres: contemptus obprobrio ad laudem d. n. I. C.

4. Innocentius de contemptu mundi 34
Capitula. Text. Domino patri karissimo
—uiuos et mortuos et seculum per ignem. Amen.
De penis inferni. In inferno secundum maiorum tradiciones.

5. Late title. Articuli Roberti lincolniensis Ep. qui floruit a°. 1242 45
Cum appropinquasset ihesus ierosolimam etc. m^t xxi. Nota quod quinque ponuntur in hoc euangelio.
The title is erroneous so far as I can see. The tract is a collection of short sermons ending f. 57 a. On 57 b are notes, inter alia:
Exemplum. Garcio querens equum in campo frenum abscondit et auenam pretendit et postea circa collum brachia ponit. et ascendit, sic etc. þe whyle þ^t ich wore gold on mi gloue. Whanne ich habbe what I wole, godes grame on þi bile.

6. Templum domini Roberti Lincolniensis (?) 58
Templum dei sanctum est
—est esse intemperancia. quod nobis prestare dignetur deus.
Expl. articuli mag. Rob. Lincoln. Ep.

7. Duodecim abusiua seculi huius (sec. B. Cyprianum: Hartel, III. 152) . . . . 66 b
—esse incipiat in futuro.

8. De vita et honestate clericorum. Capitula . . . . 67 b
Debentes de uobis rationem bonam reddere
—adiuuante I. C. canonice punituros.

9. Compilacio m. Will. de montibus cancellarii Lincoln. . . 70
Qui bene presunt presbiteri (usually attributed to Rich. Wethersett)
—hic tamen erit consummatus.
Finito libro etc.

10. (Adso) de Antichristo (P. L. cxxxvii.) . . . . 118 b
Omnes de Antichristo scire uolentes
—quod ea hora seculum iudicabit qua iudicandum tunc predixit.

Hebrew alphabet (names and meanings of letters) . . 119 *b*
11. A collection of legends under various heads . . . . f. 120
   1. Miracles of the Virgin. Fuit quidam archiepiscopus in tho-
      letana urbe. 2. Of the Cross. 3. Of Angels. 4. Of Saints.
      5. Of the Church. 6. Of Faith. 7. Of the Sacraments.
      Ending unfinished f. 152 *b*.
12. In another hand. Lessons for the Conception of the Virgin . 153 *b*
     Sermons on Gospels . . . . 155 *b*
     Legend of S. Margaret. Post passionem et resurrectionem . 158
13. Pater Noster, Aue, Credo, Confiteor, Decem precepta, vii
      peccata, In manus tuas, In nomine patris, Per crucis hoc
      signum fugit etc., Vestio cibo poto (opera misericordie),
      Forma baptismi. All in English rhyme 162
     Pater Noster begins Vre fader in heuene · yhalȝed bo þy name
         þy kynedom to us mote come for þar is
         blisse and game.
     Other verses. Boe ware soe ih boe. A day me comeþ
     sorewen þre.
     In eleuacione corporis domini, with a French verse : Sire deu
     omnipotent.
     Preces dominicales (heads of bidding prayer) . . . 163
     On riches.   Worldlih eȝte is ywonne mid svynk and svetinge
         And hit is iloked mid areȝe dredingge
         And furlete me hit schal mid soreȝe and morningge.
     In another hand.   In þe daye of seynte svythone rane ginneþ
         rinigge
         forti dawes mid ywone lestez(?) sueh tiþinge.
     Si pluat in festo processi et martiniani
     Quadraginta dies continuare solet. f. 163 *b* blank.
14. Vindicta Salvatoris (Tischendorf, *Evv. Apocr.* p. 471) . . 164
     In diebus imperii tyberii cesaris tetrarcha herode procurante
     poncio pilato iudeam traditus fuit dominus zelotus a tyberio
     —in profundum fluminis cauentes usque in hodiernum diem.
15. Letter of Prester John to Emperor Manuel . . . . 165 *b*
     Presbiter Johannes potencia et uirtute
     —repleti et refecti.   Vale.
     Verses on examples of penitence added . . . . 167 *b*
16. On the Cross.   Crux Christi conficiebatur ex quatuor lignis . 167 *b*
     Story of Pilate. Fuit quidam rex nomine cyrus . . . 167 *b*
     Story of Judas. Legitur in quadam historia . . . 168 *b*
         —demonibus sociaretur (*Legenda Aurea*, ed. Graesse,
         pp. 184, 221).
     Of Mary Magdalene. Narrat iosephus quod maria magdalene
      (death, and speech to S. Maximin) . . . . . 169 *b*
     Of S. Marina. Erat homo quidam secularis . . . 170
     Of S. Aldate. Temporibus constantini quem britanii fere
      tocius patrie uispilionum depopulacionibus exterminio co-
      gente contulerunt sibi in regem 171

—pridie nonarum febr. celebratur et colitur. ad laud. et
glor. etc. (Unpublished.)

Note added on xii genera penitencie . . . . . f. 172

17. Hic inc. statuta dominorum episcoporum Sarum . . . 172 *b*
Racionalis et proprii arbitrii factus homo.
Ends: Item necantes partum—ut qui dormiendo opprimit
partum et R. Expl.
Note from Augustine follows.

18. De negligencia presbiterorum circa altare 176
Si per negligenciam aliquid de sanguine.
Quatuor sunt cause quare seruata crux a fidelibus est...adoranda 176 *b*

19. Tractatus qui dicitur Speculum Ecclesie (Hugonis de S. Sabina) 177
Inc. tract. d. Hugonis S. Sabine Cardinalis. Dicit apostolus
ad Ephesios vi: Induite uos arma etc.
—subsequitur hominem in bonis operibus. Expl. Spec.
ecclesie.
Verses on the ten plagues etc. . . . . 180 *b*
Diffiniciones uerborum scripture 181
Diffiniciones uerborum secundum auctores.
Notes and memorial verses in a small close hand, also questions
on ritual etc. probably interesting: they develope into short
sermons 182

20. In another hand. Sermons 186
De omnibus sanctis. *Letabor ego super eloquia tua* Ps. super
eloquia diuina letandum est.
An English collection, S. Thomas of Canterbury is the only
English Saint.
Ends with the Exaltation of the Cross f. 242 *a*.

21. Ex gestis Alexii. Paciens vilia a vilibus personis tollerat.
Alexius filius fuit Eufemiani . . . . . . 242 *b*
—circa annos domini ccc. xviii. Hic et ualet ad con-
temptum mundi.
Extracts from Jac. de Vitriaco and Caesarius of Heisterbach
to show the merits and dangers of taking the Cross as a
Crusader. f. 243 *b* blank.

22. Two leaves of kalendar tables in another hand . . . 244
Kalendar for Mar. and Ap. April 3. Ricardi Ep. C. in black.
17 Dedicacio ecclesie de Sonting' (Sompting in Sussex) A. d.
m⁰. cc⁰. xlvi.
19 Alphege.
Notes in red and black. Dates of Battles of Lewes and
Evesham.
Earthquakes in England. 3 Id. Sept. 1275, hora prima, littera
dominicali F.
2 Non. Jan. 1298, in aurora, litt. domin. D (added).
18 Kal. Dec. 1318, post quartum galli cantum, litt. domin. A
(added).
Paschal tables and verses on signs f. 244 *b*, 245 *a*. On the latter

page are notes (*a*) m. cc. lxxxxvi. (*b*) ordinatio sacerdotalis
J. de chyvele. (*c*) annus gracie m. cc. nonagesimus quartus
annus regni E. Edward. 22. (*d*) Joh. du Boys viii. Id. Aug.
anno gr. m°. ccc°. xiii. litt. dom. G ortus fuit. (*e*) J. de
Tantone ortus est xi. Kal. Oct. litt. Dom. A anno gr. m°.
ccc. Sept. Brune (?).

I. 2. 7   C. M. A. 94

28. BOETHIUS DE TRINITATE.

Vellum, $9\frac{3}{8} \times 6\frac{1}{2}$, ff. 72, text 20 lines gloss 39, 40 lines to a
page. Cent. xii or xiii early, well written.

From Chichester : at bottom of f. 1 :

Boicius de Trinitate glosatus Walteri decani ii^do fo. | *quidam vero* | ꝉ. xxxvj.

Collation: 1^8-9^8.

Contents :

Prologue (of the Comment) . . . . f. 1
Libros questionum anicii quos exhortationum (*sic*) precibusque mul-
torum suscepimus explanandos.
Gloss begins f. 2. *Inuestigatam.* Premittit prologum in quo quamuis.
Text begins f. 2 *b*
Inuestigatam diutissime questionem. (*P. L.* LXIV. 124⁓.)
It is written in a narrow column on the inner side.
In xiii Thomi ending atque omnium bonorum causa (? prescribit).
Gloss ends: proposito sue uoluntatis prescribit.
Expl. Boetii Liber de Trinitate.
There are at least two hands in the volume.

I. 2. 8   C. M. A. 85

29. AUGUSTINI ETC. QUAEDAM.

Vellum, $8\frac{1}{2} \times 6\frac{1}{2}$, ff. 167 + 1, 29 lines to a page. Cent. xii early,
in a hand exceedingly like that of Christ Church Canterbury.
On the flyleaf: Tho. Leigh.   2 fo. si dicamus.
From St Étienne at Caen (Abbaye aux Hommes).
At the end of the text: Liber S. Stephani de Cadomo: qui eum
furatus fuerit uel celauerit anathema sit (xii–xiii).
On the flyleaf at end : Liber S. Stephani de caan.
Collation: 1 flyleaf. $1^4\ 2^8-12^8$ (wants 8) $13^8-21^8\ 22^4$.

On the flyleaf an original table of contents headed :

In isto uolumine sunt iste scripture.

Miscellaneous extracts follow from Aug. (on the salamander),
on adamant, the magnet, curious trees and rivers. Ending
with one on the Trinity.

I. 2. 9   C. M. A. 105

30. HERODOTUS.

Paper, 8¾ × 5⅜, ff. 326, 29 lines to a page. Cent. xv, xvi, neatly written. Red morocco binding with gold tooling, of cent. xviii. On the flyleaf is a note by Porson of which the first lines are important:

Hic liber olim Gulielmi Sancroft Archiepiscopi Cantuariensis a Thoma Galeo sed valde negligenter, longe diligentius in usum editionis Wesselingianae ab Antonio Askew collatus est ut tamen non pauca omiserit, quaedam etiam minus recte notaverit, etc.

Collation: the first two quires are in a disordered state, but the leaves have been correctly numbered (by Mr Bradshaw?). 1⁸ (wants 1 : 8 follows f. 15) 2⁸ (1 and 8 follow f. 8) 3⁸–41⁸ (wants 5). The MS. is in Cat. MSS. Angl. and cannot therefore be Askew's. Possibly it was Sancroft's as Porson suggests.

Contents :

1. On the Ionic dialect . . . . f. 2
   ἀρχὴ σὺν θεῷ τῶν ἰδιωμάτων τῆς Ἰάδος διαλέκτου.
   Ἡ Ἰὰς τὰ εἰς ᾱς λήγοντα ὀνόματα εἰς ῆς τρέπει ἐὰν μὴ ὦσι δώρια.
   Ends: φερέγγυος ὁ βεβαιωτής. ἀγηλατεύειν τὸ διώκειν. νεοχμῶσαι τὸ νεωστὶ κινῆσαί τι.

2. Herodoti Historia.
   Ἡροδότου ἱστοριῶν πρώτη 4
   Ends f. 324: ἄλλοισι δουλεύειν :
   τέλος σὺν θεῷ.
   Ἡροδότοιο βίβλος κλεινοῖο πέρας λάβεν ὡδί.

I. 2. 10   C. M. A. 104

31. DICTES AND SAYINGS OF PHILOSOPHERS.

Vellum, 8⅝ × 6½, ff. 78 + 1, 31 lines to a page. Cent. xv, well written, with nice drawings, vellum wrapper. An old number 39 on 2nd cover.

Ex dono Samuelis Starlinge quondam socii.

On f. 7 b Marie Hitchins (xvi).

Collation: 1² (wants 1) 1⁶ 2⁸ 3⁸ 4⁸ (wants 8) 5⁸–8⁸ 9⁶ 10⁸ (+ 5*) 11? (two left).

Contents :

> Dictes and Sayinges of Philosophers.
> Begins imperfectly in the sayings of Hermes :
>> from his frendeschippe as longe as thou may guide eny man to redresse hym.
> There is a coloured drawing of each philosopher at the beginning of the section devoted to him viz.
> Tat. with book.
> Zalgwynus.
> Homer.
> Solon with book and pen case.
> Zabion.
> Ipocras with doctor's vessel.
> Pitagoras.
> Dyogenes, cask on *L.* with hinged door in the side.
> Socrates.
> Platon.
> Aristotle.
> Alexandre the grete with crown and sceptre : another smaller.
> Darius twice, small.
> Two more of Alexander, one small.
> Tholomee, moon and stars above.
> Assaron with doctor's vessel.
> Legmon.
> Moder of Alexandre queen, better drawn.
> Alexander.
> Ends : for all that he may not meeake hym goode.
> There are many late scribbles on the margins : one on f. 75
>> Hec indentura facta apud watirfordiens.
> Another on f. 52 *b* is in Irish and reads : armaht nholc.
> On the same page, in an English hand, is : exemplum de villa Jernemuth in comitatu Norff.
> This last hand writes various notes opposite appropriate sayings. Thus on f. 72 *b*, à propos of an injunction not to make great buildings which others will inherit, is ...pro Johanne ffastolff (mili)te ditissimo qui (egi)t contra istud concilium. Again on f. 44 *b* : whi old peple enforceth theym to kepe theire Ritchesse... bicause that after theire dethe thei had leuer leue it to their ennemyes than to be in daunger of theire freendes. *Note :* pro J. ffastolff.
> On 45 *b* is a late scribble mentioning Richart... of bally magrir and tomas skeddy merchantt man of Corck.
> On f. 57 Thomas Jonson.

The earlier set of notes was made by some one for the purposes of sermon-making.   The book has evidently been in Ireland.   Did it belong to Bale or Bedell ?

I. 2. 11   vac.

32. THEOCRITUS ETC.

Paper, 8⅛ × 6, ff. 232, various volumes of cent. xiv? xv.

I. Two quires of 8 leaves in wrong order (2 should precede 1), seven lines to a page. The upper corner of quire 1 torn off and a hole in the inner side of all the leaves in quire 2. The margins are prepared for scholia. Cent. xv.

Theocritus. Idyll vii. 1. 124 . . . . f.   1
κοκκύσδων, νάρκαισιν ἀνιηρῇσι διδοίη.
Ends f. 3 a
δράγματα καὶ μάκωνας ἐν ἀμφοτέρῃσιν ἔχοισα.
Idyll viii. Hypothesis in smaller hand . . . . .   3 b
(Τ)ὰ μὲν πράγματα ἐν σικελίᾳ ἐστὶν
—ἀλέξανδρος δέ φησιν ὁ αἴτωλος, ὑπὸ δάφνιδος μαθεῖν
μᾶρσύλαν τὴν ἁλιευτικήν.
(Δ)άφνιδι τῷ χαρίεντι συνήντετο βουκολέοντι.
Ends imperfectly f. 8 b : καλὸν καλὸν εἶμεν ἔφασκεν (l. 76 (73)).
Followed by Idyll vii. 10 sqq.   9
Καὶ οὔπω τὰν μεσάταν ὁδὸν ἄνυμες οὐδὲ τὸ σᾶμα.
Ending f. 16 b :
μὴ δὲ πόδας τρίβωμες· ὁ δ' ὄρθριος ἄλλον ἀλέκτωρ (123).

II. Thirty leaves, 23 lines to a page, in an ugly hand of cent. xv.

A fragment of the Greek version of Boethius de Consolatione Philosophiae by Maximus Planudes: begins imperfectly in Lib. 1.
πρωτίστην πάντων τὴν ἀμείνω δόξαν τοὺς κακῶς πράσσοντας ἐξίστασθαι
καὶ ἐγκαταλείπειν.
Lib. II. begins on the 4th leaf.   Lib. III. on the 27th.
Ends imperfectly in the metre
ἵνα τῶν ὄντων ἠνί' ἐλίσσει...
εἰ καὶ δεσμὰ φέρουσι λέοντες (Lib. III. Metrum II.).

III. Thirty-one leaves, at first 24 lines to a page, then text and scholia, the former varying, the latter 46 lines to a page. In a very pretty hand of cent. xv.

Collation: a⁸ (wants 1 blank : 8 misbound) b⁸ c⁸ [here follows 8th leaf of a] d⁸. The quires are not in right order.

Lycophronis Alexandra cum commentario Isaaci Tzetzae.
Βίβλος μὲν τελέθουσα Λυκόφρονος αἱματοκόμπου
ἣν ἀλαὸς προπάροιθεν ἀδερκέα δέρματ' ἔχουσα
νῦν δέ με δορκαλέην ἑρμείη θείκατο τέχνη
τζέτζης ἰσαάκιος σύστροφα πείσματα λύσας.

Προθεωρία

τοῖς τῶν ποιητικῶν βίβλων κατάρχεσθαι μέλλουσι κ.τ.λ.

Γένος λυκόφρονος τοῦ ποιητοῦ . . . . f. 3
ὑπόθεσις . . . . 3 b
f. 5 b blank.
Text f. 6. Λέξω τὰ πάντα νητρεκῶς α μ' ἱστορεῖς . . .   6
Comment. Λέξω τὰ πάντα (in red). τοῦτο τὸ σχῆμα καὶ ὁ ποιητικὸς
τρόπος.
f. 6 has lines 1–11. ff. 7–14, ll. 28–102.
ff. 15–22, ll. 281–395. f. 23, ll. 12–17.
ff. 24–31, ll. 103–179.
Another quire is in the next volume (I. 2. 12).

IV. Forty-six leaves, 10 lines to a page. In the same hand
as no. I. Prepared for scholia.
Collation: a⁸–e⁸ f⁶.

Hesiodi Theogoniae et Scuti Herculis pars.
Quire a contains
Theogonia 520 ταύτην γάρ οἱ μοῖραν ἐδάσατο μητιέτα ζεύς
to 680   —μακρὸς ὄλυμπος.
Quire b, Theog. 846 πρηστήρων ἀνέμων
to 1006   —θέτις ἀργυρόπεζα.
Quire c, Scutum 100 φοίβου ἀπόλλωνος
to 138   —ἡρακλῆος θείοιο.
Then a space of one line at the bottom of the page followed on the
next leaf by the Hypothesis.
Μεγακλῆς ὁ ἀθηναῖος γνήσιον μὲν οἶδε τὸ ποίημα
—μιμήσασθαι τὴν ὁμήρου ἀσπίδα.
'Ιστέον ὅτι ἡ τοῦ ἡρακλέους αὕτη ἀσπὶς ἦν ἡσίοδος ἐκφράζει
—καὶ τὸν ταύτην ἐκφράσαντα ποιητήν.
Scutum 139 Χερσί γε μὴν
to 238   —τεύχε' ἔχοντες.
Quire d, Theog. 1006 γείνατ' ἀχιλλῆα to 1022 (end) διὸς αἰγιόχοιο.
The 2nd leaf blank.
ὑπόθεσις τῆς ἀσπίδος. τῆς ἀσπίδος ἡ ἀρχὴ
—γήμαντος θεμιστονόην.
Scut. 1 Ἦ οἵη προλυποῦσα—99 ἱερὸν ἄλσος.
Quire e, Theog. 681 ῥιπῇ—845 πελώρου.
Quire f, Scut. 400 οἷα διόνυσος—480 (end) δοκεύων.
One blank leaf.
In all. Theog. 520–1022. Scut. Herc. 1–238, 400–480.

The MS. was fully collated by Paley for his edition. His
symbol for it is N : he regarded the text as very good.

MS. Barocc. 60 (in the Bodleian) contains exactly that part of
the Theogony which is missing in this MS. viz. 1–519.

V.   One quire of ten leaves, 23 lines to a page, in a good hand
of cent. xv with some Latin notes, marginal and interlinear, in an
Italian hand of cent. xv.

Dionysii Periegesis.   Title in faint red ink.

Ἀρχὴ Διονυσίου περι ηδ.γητ.. (περιηγήσεως?)

Ἀρχόμενος γαῖαντε καὶ εὐρέα πόντον ἀείδειν.

Ends l. 461.—περίδρομοι εἰν ἁλὶ νῆσοι.

VI.   Twenty-five leaves in single and double columns of 19
and 24 lines, in a rough hand of cent. xv.   Three quires of 8 leaves
preceded by one detached leaf.

Poems of Gregory Nazianzen.

f. 1 end of a poem in double columns ending:

σοὶ δὲ ἐπαναπαύσαιμι τὸν βίον καὶ τὰ κακὰ παρελθὼν ἠ ἀλάξας
Εἰς ἑαυτὸν δι' ἐλεγείων.

Δύσμορος οἷα πάθον (ll. 1–11, 207–227: P. G. XXXVII. 1354).

Τοῦ θεολόγου πρὸς τοὺς ἐν κοινοβίω μοναχοὺς δι' ἐπῶν.

('Εστὶ μὲν δὴ πλεόνεσσιν ὁμὸν βίον αἰνήσαιεν.

Followed by other poems: the last εἰς ἐπισκόπους. ζωγράφος ἐστὶν
ἄριστος κ.τ.λ., 76 lines remain ending ὕβριν ἀποσκεδάσαις.

VII.   Thirty-two leaves in quires of eight, 13 and 14 lines to a
page, in a clear hand of cent. xv.

Quinti Smyrnaei Posthomerica.   Quire 1 contains 1. 1–223.

Εὖθ' ὑπὸ Πηλείωνι δάμη θεοείκελος Ἕκτωρ.—ἐντέα καλά.

Quire 2, I. 670 τοίης ἀλόχοιο, after 682 a blank page, the 2nd leaf
continues with 683.—830 ἱκέσθαι.   Then τέλος τοῦ δευτέρου
βιβλίος (sic).

A blank page.   Then II. 1–26.

Quire 3, II. 27–251, βάλε πέτρω.

Quire 4, I. 446, καὶ ταλάρους to 669 νοστήσαντες.

A further portion is in I. 2. 11.

VIII.   Sixteen leaves (two quires of eight), text and gloss (the
latter 25 lines to a full page).   Cent. xv.

Hymn on the Cross with comment, beginning and ending imperfectly: the first words of the text are

(Π)λευρᾶς ἀχράντου λόγχῃ τρωθείσης ὕδωρ σὺν αἵματι ἐξεβλύσθη.

IX.   Four leaves (proper order 1, 3, 4, 2), nine lines to a page,
cent. xv, xvi, prepared for scholia.

Sophocles Ajax 522 χάρις χάριν to 600 ἀφ' οὗ χρόνος omitting 549–556.

E. C. C.   3

X. Two leaves, the 2nd blank, 19 lines to a page.   Cent. xv.

A fragment on Grammar or Rhetoric.

Τοῦτο δὲ καταπλοκήν τινες ὠνόμασαν· ἐξαιρεῖται μὲν τὴν ὑπτιότητα
—συνθήκη δὲ γοργὴ ἡ ὀλιγάκις ἢ μηδόλως ἔχουσα.

XI. Two leaves, 25 lines to a page.   Cent. xv.   Grammatical.

Ἰστέον ὅτι τοῦ ῥήματος αἱ διαθέσεις εἰσὶ πέντε
—καὶ μετ' αὐτὸ γενικοῦ προσώπου.

XII. A quire of 8 leaves, the last four blank, 19 lines to a page. Cent. xv. On pronouns.

—τισμὸν τῶν κατὰ σύνταξιν λόγων.
Ends unfinished (on αὐτοῖς): χωρίζοντες αὐτὰ ἀπὸ τῆς ἁπλῆς ἥτις ψιλοῦται.

I. 2. 12   C. M. A. 131

33. PINDAR ETC.

Paper, 9 × 6¼, various volumes of cent. xv, ff. 118.
Collation: 1⁸ (wants 1?, 8?) 2⁸–12⁸ | 13⁸ | 14⁸ | 15⁸.

I. Pindar, *Pyth.* I. 80.

('Εκ θεῶν γὰρ μαχαναὶ πᾶ-)
σαι βροτέαις ἀρεταῖς   .   .   .   .   f.   1
Ten lines to a page, prepared for scholia. Probably formed part of the same volume as the Theocritus and Hesiod in I. 2. 11 though not in the same hand.
The text continues to *Pyth.* II. 3 (ἀνδρῶν), one leaf is lost. Continues (f. 7) ἄλλοις δέ τις (13). Up to *Pyth.* XII. 28, εἰ δέ τις ὄλβος ἐν ἀν(θρώποισιν).
Then a gap. Continues *Nem.* II. 23 (35) ἑπτὰ δ' ἐν νεμέᾳ   .   87
to the end of *Nem.* III.
δέδορκεν φάος, a blank leaf follows.
The text, according to Dr Fennell, belongs to the Moschopulean family.

II. One quire of 8 leaves from the Lycophron of which other parts are in I. 2. 11, containing lines 396 ψυχρὸν δ' ἐπ' αὐταῖς to 491 λύθρῳ with the commentary   95

III. One quire of 8 leaves, 15 lines to a page. Cent. xv. A modern title neatly written.

Incipit Γρηγορίου τοῦ θεολόγου ἐπισκόπου Ναξιανζοῦ περὶ τῶν καθ' ἑαυτὸν ἔπη δι' ὧν παροξύνει ἡμᾶς λεληθότως πρὸς τὸν ἐν Χριστῷ βίον.

A pencil note. Pessimus MS. desunt hic illic versus qui in Edit.
Hervagii Basil. 1550 reperiuntur.

Κύριε ἄναξ θεὲ ἐσ πότ' ἀειρομέναις παλάμῃσι
—ἐμὸν πόνον ἐξαγορεύσω.

IV. One quire of 8 leaves, 14 lines to a page, from the Quintus Smyrnaeus of which parts are in I. 2. 11 containing Lib. I. 224 ἔγχεα καὶ θώρηκας to 445 εἴρια θέντο.

I. 2. 13   C. M. A. 102
34. New Testament in English.

Vellum, 8½ × 5¾, ff. 207, double columns of 39 lines. Cent. xiv (1397) well written.

In the Kalendar at the end of Feb. is this note

þus þese lettres failen on lepe ȝeris at alle tymes, þis was writen in þᵉ ȝer of g. / sundai next aftir lepe ȝeer of b. In þe ȝeer of þe lord mᵒ. cccᵒ. lxxxxvij.

In the volume is a letter of thanks for the loan of the MS. from Mr Forshall, Nov. 9, 1847.

Collation: 1⁶ 2⁶ 3⁸–26⁸ 27⁴ (wants 4).

Contents :

> Here bigynneþ a calendar wiþ a reule þat techeþ to fynde þe gospels pistlis and lessouns þat ben red in chirchis bi al þe ȝeer in what bokes and chapitris þei ben in þe bible bigynnynge at aduent bifore cristemasse.
>
> Ends f. 6 b: Here enden þe Commemoracions reule of pistlis and gospels.

On the last leaf in a hand of cent. xvii–xviii.

> Iohn Wickleffe's translation of the New Testament finished Anno Dom. 1383 and this copy was written A.D. 1397 see yᵉ bottom of the Calendar in yᵉ month February and is valued at ten pounds.

A xvth cent. erased inscription above.

I. 2. 14　　　　　　　　　　　　　　　　　C. M. A. 120

35. HAMPOLE, ETC.

Paper, 8⅝ × 5¾, ff. 237, 30 lines to a page.　Cent xv, clearly written.
On f. 1, Geo. Davenport 1692.　　　　　　　2 fo. dederitis.
Collation impracticable.
Has suffered from damp.

Contents :

1. Hampole super *Oleum effusum* . . . . . . f. 1
   Oleum effusum etc. Nomen ihesu uenit in mundum
   —in celis gaudebunt. Amen. Expl. oleum effusum
   secundum Hampoll.
2. Hampole super hunc psalmum . . . . . . 19 *b*
   Iudica me deus etc. A deo qui scrutatur
   —uidetur uitam interrumpere. Expl. fructuosus tract. Ric.
   Hampole heremite.
3. Hampole de Actiua uita et contemplatiua 23
   Mulierem fortem etc. Quanto aurum argento
   —a recta uia uariatur.
4. (Hampole) de causa hereticorum et fide trinitatis . . . 25
   Abundancia veritatis integre
   —breui labore facit (?) sustinentes.
   Tabula huius libri additur per mag. Joh. Neuton . . 59
5. Exposicio orationis dominice per R. H. heremitum . . 61
   Pater noster etc. Hec oratio priuilegiata est
   —confirmata in veritate.
6. Liber qui uocatur Incendium Amoris sec. Ric. Hampull . 63
   Admirabar amplius quam enuncio
   —saluus etc. Amen. Expl. Incendium amoris. ff. 99 *b*
   blank.
7. Augustinus de uera uita 100
   Sapiencia dei
   —bonum perducat. Amen. Expl. Aug. de uera uita.
8. Meditaciones ymaginis uite 124
   Flecto genua mea
   —trius et unus benedictus in secula. Amen. Expl. meditaciones ymag. uite sec. Bonauenturam.
9. Tract mutilated at the beginning (one leaf gone ?) . . 164
   Ardencia illuminat illuminata
   —commendo sine fine Amen (f. 191).
   The names Michael and Anna Purefoy and Thomas ffawnte
   are scribbled on ff. 191, 192. ff. 191 *b*—193 were blank.
10. Hampole in libro qui uocatur melum amoris . . . 194
    Postquam sponsa dixerat.
    (f. 229 left blank.)
    Ends imperfectly (?). f. 237 *b* in chapter 58.

I. 2. 15 and I. 3. 13

$\left\{ \begin{array}{l} \text{I. vac. ?} \\ \text{II. ?C. M. A. } 96 \end{array} \right.$

36. MACER, ETC.

Vellum, $8\frac{1}{2} \times 6\frac{3}{8}$, ff. 43, 29 lines to a page. Cent. xiv.
Paper, $8\frac{5}{8} \times 5\frac{3}{4}$, ff. 63, 29 lines to a page. Cent. xv ?.
Collation: I. 1^{10} 2^{12} 3^{12} 4^8 (wants 7, 8): a smaller quire of 4 leaves, wanting 4.
II. 1^{14} 2^{14} (and 1) 3^{20} 4^{12} (12 a fragment).

Contents :

I. 2. 16   C. M. A. 5

37. CHRYSOSTOMUS.

Vellum, $8\frac{1}{2} \times 5\frac{3}{4}$, ff. 88, 28 lines to a page. Cent. xv, clearly written.   2 fo. Non ergo.

Given by George Barcroft, Ecclesiae Cathedralis Eliensis Ἀρχέχορος (= Precentor ?), A.D. 1597. Mart. 5°.

On the flyleaf an old title, and

> George Barcroft. A malo fuge et fac bonum.

Collation: a² 1⁸ 2⁸ (wants 2) 3⁸–10⁸ 11¹⁰ (wants 10).

Contents :

Followed by Barcroft's inscription again.

I. 2. 17   C. M. A. 7

38. Isidorus super Pentateuchum.

Vellum, 9 × 5⅝, ff. 79 + 3, 36 lines to a page. Cent. xii, very well written.

From Pershore Abbey. Two letters about the Convent are on the flyleaves.

On f. 1 at top,

> Isidorus super v. libros Moysi. Liber Gilleberti p' (prioris).

Collation: a⁴ (wants 1) 1⁸–10⁸ (wants 8).

On the flyleaves :

1. A cure for the above. Fecit (? Recipe) puluerem saxifrage etc.
2. Epitaph. Tu prope qui transis nec dicis a...o resiste
   Auribus et mente tu mea uerba tene etc.
3. In quibus emuli detrahebant S. Thome martiri.
4. Epitaph (of Petrus Comestor). Petrus eram quem petra tegit etc.
5. Dialogue in verse on the Crucifixion . . . . . f. 1 b
   Fili. quid mater. deus es. sum. cur ita pendes etc.
   Ends: A dum transit in e qui clamat ue recipit ue.

6. Versus de Archiepiscopo Vienne qui postea factus est papa
   Romanus . . . . f. 2
      Sponsum sponsa suum concessit filia matri
         Mater eum rapuit. fecit eam uiduam
      Alter habuit (habebit) eam forsan uiuente priore
         Nec de quattuor his ullus adulter erit.
   Verses on Ernulfus (6).
                        mille
      Non ernulfe locus non homo sophismata prosunt.
   Epigram. Quem recitas meus est o fidentine libellus.
   Quare sine libro loqui non debet quis in claustro (3 lines).
      Dignum promat opus frater liber aut teneatur.
   De signis metallorum (2 lines).
   De abbatibus qui ferunt anulos et mitram et sandalia (4 lines).
      Ars asino summisit equam mixturaque mulum.
   De genealogia (6 lines).
      Vulpis (Vulpe) salitur ouis dum densis uepribus heret.
      Hoc genitos ligures fabula stirpe refert.
   Hec sunt decem nociua oculis. Primus obest oculis etc. .   2 b

7. Letter from T(homas), Abp of Canterbury, to the Convent of
   Pershore, restoring their Abbot Thomas.

8. Letter of the Convent of Pershore to Bishop S. asking that
   their church may no longer be left widowed.
   Title illegible (6 lines).
      Si foret ex equo quemquam lugere uirorum
         Pre multis aliis iste dolendus erat etc.
   f. 3 b blank.
   Text. Inc. prefacio Ysidori b. Gregorii pape discipuli Yspa-
   lensis Ep. (XCIII. 417)   1
      Hystoria sacre legis non sine aliqua prenuntiatione
      —eloquenti Gregorio. Expl. pref.
   Inc. Capitula in libro Genesis.
   Inc. de libro Genesis premissio operis ab exordio mundi etc.   1 b
      Creatura celi et terre.
   Exodus 28 b. Leuit. 41. Num. 47. Deut. 54 b.
   Iosue 59 b (by Bede P. L. XCIII. 417).
   Iud. 63. 1 Reg. 68. 2 Reg. 75. 3 Reg. 76 b.
   Ends f. 79 b: qui nos a peccato mundaret (c. VII.).
   Decrees of a Council in London, in another hand . .   79 b
   Anno ab incarnatione M.C. XXXVIII. etc.
      i. Interdicimus ut pro crismate pro oleo.
      xvi. Magistri scolarum si aliis scolis suas regendas com-
      miserint.

I. 2. 18   C. M. A. 28

39. Pseudo-Chrysostomi Opus imperfectum.

Vellum, 8½ × 5⅞, ff. 260, double columns of 34 lines.   Cent. xv,
fairly well written.   2 fo. comprehensus or Abymelech.
Late names, Richard Bloxom etc., on flyleaf at end G. Davenport.
Collation: 1¹² 2⁸–32⁸.

Contents:

1. Table. Abraham—Zona.
2. Chrysostomi (Pseudo-) opus imperfectum in Matthaeum   . f.   13
   Sicut referunt quidam (*P. G.* LVI. 601).
   Ends f. 258: stantem in loco sancto. Expl. Omelie Joh.
   Crisostomi patriarche constantinopolitani super matheum.
   A later note on Daniel's prophecy of the weeks.
   Table of the Homilies . . . .   258 *b*
   Table of the Liturgical Gospels treated in the Homilies .   259 *b*

I. 2. 19   C. M. A. 412

40. Thomae Aquinatis quaedam.

Vellum, 7⅜ × 5¼, ff. 163 + 2, double columns of 25 lines.
Cent. xiii, xiv, well written.

Ex dono Rodolphi Cudworthi eiusdem Coll. socii A. d. 1600.

On the flyleaf

Iste liber est fratris a*n*to*n*ioli de p̆eraneg*in*o ordinis fratrum (erased).

Also an old table of contents headed:

In isto uolumine continentur isti tractatus per ordinem quos fecit S. Thomas de
aquino ordinis predicatorum.

Collation: a² 1¹² (wants 1) 2¹²–11¹² 12¹⁶ 13¹⁰ 14⁶.

Contents:

1. S. Thomas de fide spe et caritate, qui alio nomine appellatur
   compendium theologie sancte fidei catholice   .   .   . f.   1
   Begins imperfectly in c. 4.
   Ends f. 119: difficilius fuit.
2. Inc. tract. eiusdem fr. Thome de acquino ordinis predicatorum
   de rationibus fidei. Prohemium c. 1   119

Beatus petrus apostolus
—diligencius pertractata sunt.
3. Inc. tract. de articulis fidei secundum fr. Th. de aquino ord.
    pred. . . . . f. 135 *b*
    Postulat a me uestra dileccio
    —sub alio voluntatem. Expl. tract. fr. Th. de art. fidei.
4. Inc. tract. de sacramentis ecclesie fr. Thome . . . 142 *b*
    Hiis uisis circa ecclesie sacramenta
    —christus dei filius. Amen. Expl. de sacramentis.
    Supplement of an omitted passage in no. 3. . . . 146 *b*
5. Tract. fr. Thome in quibus licet uti iudicio astrorum . . 147
    Quia petisti ut tibi
    —iudiciis astrorum uti. Expl.
6. Tract. eiusdem fr. Thome de forma absolucionis in confessione
    sacramentali . . . . 147 *b*
    Perlecto libello
    —compillans laborarem. Expl.
7. Tract. eiusdem fr. Thome de occultis operibus nature . . 153
    Quoniam in quibusdam naturalibus
    —dicta sufficiant. Expl.
8. Tract. eiusdem fr. Thome de motu cordis . . . . 155 *b*
    Quia omne quod mouetur.
    Ends f. 160 *b*: uidentur probabilitatem afferre. Expl.
    In the table two more titles follow of tracts not in the volume, viz.
    de mixtione elementorum in mixto.
    de eternitate mundi.
    Capitula of the first two tracts.

I. 2. 20   C. M. A. 122

41. HORAE.

Vellum, 7⅜ × 5¼, ff. 69, 23 lines to a page.   Cent. xv, well written.
Coarse pictures.

Collated by Mr Bradshaw. (m) one left n⁸ (+ 7*) o⁸ p⁸ (+ 3*) q⁸
r⁸ (+ 5*6*7*) s⁸ (+ 6*) t⁸ (+ 3*) v⁸? (wants 1, 8).

Contents :

Seven Joys of the Virgin. Rubric. Quicunque hec septem gaudia etc. f.   1
    Virgo templum trinitatis.
O domina glorie . . . . 2 *b*
Ad ymaginem Christi crucifixi: Omnibus consideratis . . . 3
    Prayer to the Cross and Five Wounds.
Ad uirginem Mariam. O Maria plasma nati 4
Ad S. Johannem euuang. Johannes euuangelista.
        tu sacrarii sacrista . . . . 4 *b*

On f. 22 *a* is a xvith cent. scribble that Martin Crugh (?) owes
Roger of Drougheda £5. 6s. 3d.

The following pictures occur :

1. Initial f. 1. Pietà. Two figures : the cross behind.
2. f. 3—The Fall. 3. f. 3 *b*. The Three Crosses. 4. The Holy Face;
red ground.
5. The Right Hand of Christ: blue ground. 6. The Left Hand.
7. The Five Wounds. 8. The Right Foot. 9. The Left Foot.
10. Virgin and Child seated : a wall behind. 11. St John with cup, in a room.
12. f. 5. The Crucifixion with the Virgin and St John.
13. Full page. *Seven Psalms.* Christ as Judge on the rainbow. The Virgin and
John Evangelist kneel on earth : five dead people rise. Two angels in air with Trumpets.
14. Full page. *Office of the Dead.* Christ on *L.* attended by Mary (Magd.) and
John. Lazarus stepping out of a grave in the earth. Two Jews on *R.* Background of
buildings.
15. *Prayers.* f. 39. Full page. Mass of St Gregory. He kneels at altar on *L.*
on which stands Christ supporting the Cross. A server kneels on *L.* Two Cardinals
on *R.* hold the tiara and crozier.
16. *Commendationes.* Full page. Two angels stand on earth by two graves
holding between them a cloth in which are two nimbed souls. Christ and angels in
the sky.
17. *Psalms of the Passion.* Full page. The Man of Sorrows, half-length on blue
cloud, over the tomb. Behind and above on red ground the instruments of the Passion,
including busts of Pilate (?), Caiaphas (?), Annas (?) and Peter.
18. *Psalter of St Jerome.* Full page. Jerome as Cardinal seated in vaulted room.
Desk on *R.* Lion at his feet.
  The Litany has traces of Flemish influence. *Martyrs:* Adrian, Potentian, Thomas,
Edward, Oswald, Alanus, Lambert, Julian. *Confessors:* Hubert, Remigius, Bavo,
Vedastus, Columba, Philibert, Botulph, Amandus. *Virgins:* Genovefa, Susanna, Editha.

I. 2. 21
42.

Paper, 7⅜ × 6⅞, pp. 479 numbered: more than half blank. Cent. xvii, well written.

Extracts and notes for Sermons.
Dominica Iᵃ post Pentecosten.
Estote misericordes.

The extracts are from Stapleton, Coster, Peraldus etc.: at p. 428 is part of a Table.

I. 2. 22
43.

Paper, 7½ × 6, pp. 485 numbered. Cent. xvii, in the same hand as the last.

A book of Extracts on various topics, probably for use in Sermons.
A list of subjects after p. 482.

I. 2. 23
44.

Paper, 7½ × 5¾, ff. circ. 150. Cent. xvii, very finely written, dark leather binding with gold tooling.

Treatise on Predestination.
The Preface to my Worthy Freind and reverend Pastor perswading to peace and mutuall Tolerancie.
Analytical Table.
The First opinion.
The order of Gods Predestination according to the opinion of Mr Calvin, Mr Beza and their followers.
The book was written after the death of James I who is referred to as "our late Soueraigne."
Three opinions are treated. No author's name seems to occur in the MS.

I. 2. 24
45.

Paper, 7⅜ × 4¾, ff. circ. 100. Cent. xvii, clearly written.
Given by Abp Sancroft whose name is on f. 1.

On the flyleaf are some notes

The Title of ye first Book in ye original.

Acta Convocationis de Suprematu Regio in Ecclesiasticis: quodque Suprematum talem potestates supremae in Ecclesia Dei jam inde ab Adamo ad Christum exercuerunt.

Then a version of the Title by Abp Laud, and other notes. On the verso in Sancroft's hand: Junii 24° 1689. Jmprimatur. W. Cant.

Tis endorst. Bp Overal's Convocation Book 1606.
Title of ye whole Book. Concerning ye Government of God's Catholick Church and ye kingdomes of ye whole World.

It is evidently a copy made for the press, and was printed in London in 1690.

I. 2. 25   ? vac.

46. Tractatus de Decalogo etc.

Vellum, 7 × 4⅝, ff. 90, 27 lines to a page. Cent. xv. Two volumes.

Title in the cover written by Dr Farmer:

Homiliae in Decalogum cum Directorio Sacerdotum.

Collation: 1^10–4^10 (wants 10) ‖ 5^12 (12 canc.?) 6^10–8^10 (wants 10) 9^10 (+ 1).

Contents:

I. 1. Sermons on the Commandments . . . . . f. 1
        Si uis ad uitam ingredi serua mandata. Mt. 19. Dicturi de preceptis uideamus primo.
        Ends f. 31 b: reliqua ad omnes homines communiter.
        Expl. tract. de decem mandatis.
    2. On hindrances to prayer . . . . . . 31 b
        Primum impedimentum quare oratio non auditur etc.
    3. Bonauentura de decem mandatis 33
        Si uis ad uitam etc. Verba ista in matheo et sunt saluatoris nostri.
        Ends imperfectly 39 b: affirmatiua sed in nouo testamen(to).
II.   A Directorium Sacerdotum for the year: apparently of Sarum Use 40
        Begins imperfectly (one quire at least being lost) in Littera Dominicalis B.
        Ends f. 90 a with Letter G.
        There are a good many variations of hand in Vol. I, and scribbles of cent. xvi, which do not seem interesting.

I. 2. 26

47. ANT. ASKEW'S ALBUM AMICORUM.

Vellum and paper, $7\frac{1}{8} \times 4\frac{1}{2}$, ff. circ. 50, many blank.   Cent. xviii.
Vellum binding with gold tooling.   Title written by Dr Farmer.

Album containing complimentary mottoes etc. written for Dr Askew
in the years 1746, 1747, in Germany, Austria and Constantinople,
by various scholars including Chr. Bened. Michaelis, Joh. Matth.
Gesner, Jo. Aug. Ernesti, Jac. Burckhard, J. G. Walther etc.

I. 2. 27

48.

Paper, $7\frac{1}{2} \times 5\frac{3}{4}$, ff. 35 written.   Cent. xvii, ff. 1–30, in a beautiful
hand, possibly that of a professional scribe.

1. Dr Richard Holdsworth's Directions for Students at the
    Universities.
    General Directions 1, 2, Synopsis of Studies for four years 3–6.
    Notes on the Synopsis, and List of Books to be read 7–22.
    Further Directions about Studies 22 *b*–26.   General Directions,
    warning against Idleness and Bad Company 27–30.
2. Ex Codice D^ris Linnet Vice-Magistri Trin. Coll. Camb.
    On the office of the Regius Professors of Divinity, Hebrew
    and Greek 31–35.
    Richard Holdsworth was Master 1637–43.

I. 2. 28 Printed.   Belonged to Sir Walter Mildmay.

I. 2. 29

49.

Paper, $7\frac{7}{8} \times 8\frac{3}{4}$, ff. circ. 70.   Cent. xvii, very neatly written.

Hebrew Grammar in Latin Verse (by Joshua Barnes?).
Σὺν Θεῷ.
Hebraicae linguae studiosae juventuti animi alacritatem successusque
    a Deo prosperrimos.
        Si cupis optatam, juvenis, contingere metam,
        Et tibi letifico studium Colophone beari,
        Quotidie Deus est per Cristum in vota vocandus etc.

I. 2. 30   C. M. A. 130

50.

Paper, 8⅝ × 7, pp. 52 written, more blank.   Cent. xvii, in a good
hand.   Vellum wrapper.

Leander, Comoedia.

The cast precedes the text.

Gerastus senex   Dˢ Kitchin etc.

I. 2. 31   C. M. A. 73

51.

Paper, 8⅝ × 6¾, ff. 18 written, as many blank.   Cent. xvii,
clearly written.

1. Tract on Fortifications in French.
        Des fortifications, ff. 11.
    Ce qui a esmeu les premiers hommes a se fortifier.
2. Des feus d'artifice, 5 ff.
    Premierement pour faire les gren(a)des a feu.
3. De la sphaire, ff. 2.
    Notez qu'en la sphaire il ny a que dix cercles.

All three tracts have rough diagrams.   On a subsequent page
is a heading " De l'usage du globe," but no text.

I. 2. 32

52.

Paper, 9⅛ × 7, ff. circ. 50.   Cent. xvii, well written.
Belonged to Abp Sancroft, whose name is on the first page.

Valetudinarium.   Comoedia acta coram Academicis Febr. 6° 1637,
    Authore mʳᵒ Guill. Johnson Coll. Regin. Soc.

I. 2. 33

53.

Paper, 9 × 6⅝. ff. circ. 100.   Cent. xvi late.

The Names of the Justices of Peace and Deputy Lieutenants in all
    the Counties of England and Wales A.D. 1595.
Followed by the Circuits of the Justices of Assize 14 Aug. 1595.

The names of the Sheriffs 1595. Lieutenants and Deputy-
Lieutenants. Commissioners for Musters.
March 1596. Abstract of the forces...furnished by the Clergie.
Soldiers levyed in various counties in June 1594 and sent into
Ireland then.
Further particulars of forces sent into Ireland, France, and the
Low Countries in 1594–1599.
Oathe of one of the priuie Counsell.
Oathe of the Secretaries or Counsailors.

I. 3. 1   C. M. A. 83
54. SOLILOQUIA AUGUSTINI ETC.

Vellum, 8 × 5⅛, ff. 139 + 1, 31 lines to a page. Cent. xv, well
written.   2 fo. illumina.
At end
            Liber Rogeri Ched. prec. xii^d (xv).

Collation: 1 flyleaf. 1⁸–4⁸ | 5⁸–14⁸ | 15⁸–17⁸ 18⁴ (wants 4): old
foliation incorrect but I make use of it.
There is an erasure of two lines on the flyleaf.

Contents:

I.   1. Liber soliloquiorum S. Augustini. (*P. L.* XXXII. 869) . f.   1
         Agnoscam te domine
             —ut aquile annos meos.
II. 2. Musica ecclesiastica de imitacione Christi et contemptu
         omnium uanitatum   34
         Qui sequitur me
             —ecclesie sacrosancto et fui ipsius etc.
         f. 113 blank.
III.   Speculum S. Edmundi (*Bibl. Patr. Lat.* Tom. XXV. p. 316)   114
         Begins imperfectly in c. 1.
         die ac nocte ex una parte habeo magnum gaudium
             —paratum ab origine mundi. Amen.
         Expl. tract. S. Edmundi de Pontiniaco qui appellatur
         speculum ecclesie et bene potest ita nominari cum in
         tota sacra sciptura non poterit aliquid specialius inueniri.

I. 3. 2
55.

Paper, 8 × 6¼, ff. circ. 100. Cent. xvii early, very neatly written.

A common-place book containing notes and extracts from Petrarch, Jos. Scaliger,
Fynes Morison's Itinerary, various classical authors and Platina.

On one leaf in English near the end are notes of a "relation of Anthony Knivet" of perils undergone by him in South America and Africa.

Earlier in the volume are some pages beginning with " my lord keepers judgement" on the Earl of Essex, and going on with a character of some politician who lived in Ireland and died in 1606.

I. 3. 3   C. M. A. 87

56. HIERONYMUS CONTRA JOVINIANUM ETC.

Vellum, $8\frac{1}{8} \times 6\frac{3}{8}$, ff. 158 + 4, mostly double columns of 34 lines. Cent. xv and xiii.

Given in 1667 by Tho. Leigh, S. Th. B. nuper socius.

2 fo. de una.

On f. 158 b

Mag. Joannis Veysy ex donacione......(xv, xvi).

At the end are various names

John Wyse, Ffrauncis Cope.   Erasure of $3\frac{1}{2}$ lines.

Collation: a^2 1^8–13^8 | 14^8–17^8 18$^?$ (two) | 19^{12} 20^{12} (wants 11, 12): b^2. An old table of contents on f. ii b headed

In hoc uolumine continentur hec uidelicet.

Contents :

Rescriptum eiusdem Jeronimi (Tischendorf *Evv. Apocr.*
p. 51).

Jeronimus exiguus christi seruus . . . . . f. 85
which passes without a break into the Liber de natiuitate
b. Marie (Tischendorf *Evv. Apocr.* p. 113).
—regnat deus per omnia sec. sec. Amen. Expl. Jeron.
de natiu. b. M. V. Deo gracias.

4. Inc. pref. b. Augustini Ep. in tractatum de assumpcione
b. Virginis . . . . 88 *b*
Ad interrogata de virginis et matris domini (XL. 1141).
Inc. tract. b. Augustini Ep. de assumpcione b. Virginis . 89
Quia profundissime.

5. Sermons of St John Chrysostom viz.
de ieiunio Niniuitarum in letania. Clementissimus
omnipotens deus 93
de milicia spirituali. Bona quidem sunt . . 95
de milicia christiana. Omnes homines qui se . 97
de muliere mala. Heu me quid agam . . 99 *b*
de muliere bona. Sed hactenus mihi . . 101 *b*
f. 104 blank.

II. 6. In a later hand.
Expositio Jeronimi super Marcum (XXX. 560) . . 105
Omnis scriba doctus in regno
—luca concordans enarrat. Expl. exp. Jeron. super
marcum.

7. Continuacio noui et ueteris testamenti (attributed to St
Ambrose *P. L.* XV. 1961) 128
Continuare uolumus quedam que dicit Josephus
—iam finis erit operi legenti ne sit oneri.

III. 8. In a fine hand of cent. xiii, in triple columns.
Inc. descriptio eusebii ieronimi de formulis hebraicarum
litterarum que dextrorsum etc. with Hebrew letters
(XXXII. 1305?) 139
Prefatio Ieronimi in libro interpr. hebr. nominum.
Philo uir disertissimus (XXIII. 771).
Inc. liber interpr. hebr. nominum. Non statuis ubicunque.
Interpr. nominum de genesi etc. Aethiopie tenebre.
Ends : de epistola barnabe. Sathan aduersarius etc.

9. Inc. pref. Jeronimi in libro locorum ab eusebio...edito . 148 *b*
Eusebius qui a b. phamphilo (XXIII. 859).
Ararath—Zoeleth.
Expl. lib. S. Jeron. presb. de locis.

I. 3. 4   C. M. A. 87

57. HIERONYMUS DE LOCIS ETC.

Vellum, 8⅛ × 5⅝, ff. 166 + 2, mostly 30 (and more) lines to a page.
Cent. xii early, in several excellent hands.   2 fo. mons nomine.

Given by Tho. Leigh in 1667.

On the flyleaf:

Henricus Gocheus.

Collation: 1 flyleaf.   1⁸–5⁸ | 6⁸–20⁸ 21⁶ | 1 flyleaf.

Contents :

With insertion of glose septime ebdomade beginning
Non ad hoc abbreuiauit illos annos
　　—anni solares cccclxxv.
Ends with Diotrepes (3 Jo.).
12. Inc. de spera celi et de diuersis scripturis　.　.　. f. 109
Affirmatur celum rotundum
　　—audisti me cui obedisti liberet te.　f. 112 b blank.
13. In another hand.　Epistles of Jerome and Augustine.
　　1. Jeron. ad Tranquillinum (de Origene, Ep. 62 : XXII.
　　606).　2. Aug. ad Jeron. (XXXIII. 720).
　　3. Rescriptum Jeron.　4. Item Jeron. ad Aug.
　　5. Aug. ad Presidium.
　　6—12.　Aug. ad Jeron. et Jer. ad Aug.　de origine anime.
　　13.　Explanatio fidei S. Jeron.　Credimus in deum patrem.
　　14.　Disputatio de ratione anime.　Cum apud uos celestis.
　　15.　Jer. ad Paulinum.　16.　Jer. Amando.
　　17.　Exemplarii Responsio.
　　18.　Pammachius et Oceanus Jeronimo.
　　19.　Jeron. Pammachio.
　　20.　Jer. ad Oceanum de uita clericorum.
　　21.　Epiphanius ad Johannem CPol.
　　22.　Jeron. ad Rufinum de iudicio Salomonis.
　　23.　Ad Vitalem.　24.　Ad Castricianum.
　　25.　Ad Domnionem.　26.　Ad Asellam.
　　27.　Ad Marcellam de v questionibus.
　　28—33.　Ad Marcellam.　34. Jeronimus .　.　.　161
Cum essem iuuenis miro discendi ferebar ardore
　　—festuca peccati non posset incidere.
f. 165 a blank.
Paragraphs: Duo sunt genera omnium rerum　.　. 165 b
　　　　　　Quia igitur sunt multe et uarie actiones ani-
　　　　　　malium.
　　　　　　Ad paralisim potio　.　.　.　.　. 166
Table of contents of cent. xv headed
　　Contenta in hoc libro.　prec. huius libri xxvjˢ. viijᵈ.

I. 3. 5   C. M. A. 119

58. Variae Lectiones in N.T.

Paper, 8 × 6⅛, ff. circ. 120.　Cent. xvii early, well written.
Given by Tho. Leigh.

A collation of the Elzevir text of the New Testament (Lugd. 1624)
with four MSS. viz.
　A.　Quatuor Evangelia MS. in Coll. Gonvillii et Caii (= Gonv.
　　　and Cai. MS. 403).

B. The Codex Bezae.
C. Evangelia MS. Henrici Googe S.T.D. et Coll. S. Trin.
    apud Cantabr. nuper Socii.
D. Nov. Test. recentiore manu descriptum quod olim fuerat
    fratris froysel (Froy Franciscani) postea Th.
    Clementis deinde Guil. Chark nunc Thomae Montfortii (=the Codex
    Montfortianus at Dublin).
    The collation comprises the four gospels and Acts i–xxii. 29.

I. 3. 6   C. M. A. 8, 80

59. PHILIPPUS SOLITARIUS ETC.

Paper, $7\frac{7}{8} \times 5\frac{1}{4}$, ff. 159, 30 lines to a page. Cent. xiv, very
neatly written.
On f. 1

Hugo Broughton D.

Collation: modern flyleaves. 1^8 (wants 1) 2^8–18^8 19^6 20^6 21^4.
Notes, on the flyleaves, on Philippus Solitarius, and the first
leaf recopied (xvii).

Contents :

1. Μερικὴ ὑπόθεσις καὶ ὑπόμνησις διὰ στιχοπλοκίας πῶς ἡ ψυχὴ τοῦ
    σώματος διαζεύγνυται......
    Ἰωάννου α... καὶ ξένου δι' ὧν καὶ ἀπελέγετο πρὸς τὴν ἰδίαν ψυχήν·
    στίχοι τῆ .   .   .   . f. 1
    Πῶς κάθη πῶς ἀμεριμνεῖς, πῶς ἀμελεῖς ψυχή μου
                          ...
    Ἀμὴν ἀμὴν χριστός μου γένοιτο γένοιτό μοι.
    Edited from this MS. by Dr E. S. Shuckburgh.
    It was formerly regarded as the first book of the Dioptra of
    Philippus Solitarius.
    Lib. II. begins f. 8
    (Τ)ὰ δὲ ἐστὶν ἐν τῷ δευτέρῳ λόγῳ.
    Πολλοὺς μὲν ἔχομεν ὁμοῦ καὶ χρόνους καὶ καιρούς τε.
    Lib. III. f. 34 b. Lib. IV. f. 65. Lib. V. f. 89.
    Ending f. 153 b
    Καὶ σῶσόν με μακρόθυμε μὴ εἰς τέλος ὀλέσθαι
    Δόξα κυρίῳ τῷ θεῷ παντότε εἰς αἰώνας.
    Several quires are misbound: notes of cent. xvii show the
    right order.
2. Τοῦ ἐν ἁγίοις πατρὸς ἡμῶν Ἰωάννου ἀρχ. κωνστ. τοῦ χρυσοστόμου
    λόγος εἰς τὰ βαΐα .   .   .   . 153 b
    Ἤδη τῆς δεσποτικῆς (Savile VII. 334).
    Ends imperfectly f. 158 b.

Imperfect capitula to the Dioptra (?) in another hand . . f. 159
Scribbles in Greek and Hebrew on the verso.
The Cat. MSS. Angl. adds
   Homilia Gregorii Nyssae Ep. de generatione Jesu Christi
   et de eius Baptismo, liber fine mutilus.
But I do not detect any part of this in the MS.
It seem to be entered twice in Cat. MSS. Angl. viz.
No. 8. 1. Rhythmi Graeci de anima et corpore. Princip.
μετρικὴ ὑπόθεσις.
     2. Hom. Chrysostomi in dominica palmarum Gr.
     3. Hom. Greg. Nyssae Ep. etc. (as above).
No. 80. Διόπτρα ψυχῆς. Vetus MS. titulari pagina caret,
Chartac. 4to.

I. 3. 7   C. M. A. 11

60. MANUALE CONFESSORUM.

Vellum, $7\frac{1}{4} \times 5$, ff. 219+4, 2 columns of 41 lines. Cent. xiv,
clearly written.
On the last page:
   Iste liber constat d^{no} Johanni bayntun vicario de why^{to}.

Given by Tho. Leigh (S.T.B. nuper Socius) in 1667.
Collation: 2 flyleaves. 1^{12}–6^{12} 7^6 (+a slip) 8^{12}–$11^{10 \text{ or } 12}$ (? wants
1 and 12) 12^{12} (wants 1) 13^{12} (+a slip) 14^{12}–19^{12}: 2 flyleaves.

Contents:
(Manuale confessorum excerpta de Summa Raymundi).
Cum summa confessorum pro mā uos specialiter dirigens ob sui
   magnitudinem . . . . f. 1
   —per ordinem supponendo.
List of headings 1
Text. (S)imonia secundum theologos et iuristas diffinitur.
Ends f. 193 b: utile uel necessarium iudicabis.
Tabula. Si complete non inueneris . . . . . . 193 b
   From Abbas to Irregularis ending imperfectly.
A slip is tacked on to the last leaf containing the list of headings
to Votum.

I. 3. 8   C. M. A. 132

61. ARISTIDES DE MUSICA.

Paper, $7\frac{1}{2} \times 6\frac{7}{8}$, ff. 87 written, 23 lines to a page. Cent. xvii,
well written.

On p. 1 etc. Almae Matri EMMANVEL D.D. Josua Barnes, 1694.

> Ἀριστείδου τοῦ Κοιντιλιανοῦ
> περὶ Μουσικῆς . . . . f. 1
> Ἀλεὶ μὲν ἐμοὶ θαυμάζειν ἔπεισι.

Ends f. 87 a μιᾷ καταθέσθαι πραγματείᾳ. τέλος.
Titles, diagrams etc. are inserted in pencil only.

I. 3. 9   C. M. A. 82

62. SUMMA RAYMUNDI DE PENNAFORTI.

Vellum, $8\frac{1}{4} \times 5\frac{1}{2}$, ff. 482, double columns of 19 lines. Cent. xiii–xiv?, in a large bold cursive hand, mutilated at each end.

Collation: 1^{12} (wants 1–3) 2^{12}–26^{18} 27^{16} 28^{12}–35^{12} 36^{16}–38^{16} 39^{14} (wants 14).

On the margin of f. 398 *b* in a large hand is written Richard harewel (xv).

Contents:

> Summa Confessorum Raymundi.
> Lib. I. begins imperfectly de Symonia.
> Lib. II. f. 114. de homicidio etc.
> In prima parte dictum est de quibusdam criminibus que principaliter in deum committuntur.
> Lib. III. f. 286. de qualitate ordinandorum etc.
> Expeditis per gratiam dei duabus particulis.
> Lib. IV. f. 419. de matrimonio.
> Expeditis autem iam per dei gratiam non me. Quoniam frequenter in foro penitentiali dubitationes circa matrimonium.
> Ends imperfectly.

I. 3. 10   vac.
63.

Paper, $8\frac{1}{8} \times 6\frac{1}{4}$, pp. 77, 27 lines to a page. Cent. xvii, clearly written.

Belonged to Abp Sancroft whose name is on the title page.

> Testamentum 12. Patriarcharum Graece.
> It was Mr Jo. Gregories. I bought it of Dr Gurgeries (?) widow. Transscrib'd (as I have heard) from a MS. in y^e Bennett Coll. (lined through) University Library in Cambridge and since compar'd wth it and ye divers Readings inserted wth several supplies and additions by Dr Battelie's procurem^t who hath a fair Copie of ye whole.
> The various readings of the Bodleian MS.? are inserted in the margin.

I. 3. 11   C. M. A. ?

64. BREVIARIUM (Dublin).

Vellum, 7¾ × 5, ff. 523, double columns of 37 lines.   Cent. xv
early, excellent writing and ornaments.
On f. 251 at end of Proper of Time:

> Iste liber constat Thome Pecoke capellano (xv).

Collation: 1⁸–21⁸ 22⁶ 23⁸ (wants 1) 24⁸ (wants 1) 25⁸ (wants 3)
26⁸–39⁸ 40¹⁰ 41⁸ 42⁸ 43¹² (+ 1) 44⁸–64⁸ 65¹⁰.

Contents:

The book is a Sarum Breviary with Dublin feasts inserted in the
Kalendar, but no Dublin offices in the text so far as I can see,
and nothing Irish in the Litany.

The Kalendar contains the following entries:

Jan. 31. S. Edani Ep. C. ix lect. per co. Dublinie in red added.
Feb. 17. S. Fintani Abb.....................Dublinie ,,   ,,
     27. Added in margin Mūne ep. ix lect.
     29.   ,,   ,,   Oswaldi ep. ix lect.
Mar. 1, 2. David and Chad orig. in red.
      3. Magri Abb. added in black.
     11. Liberi Abb.   ,,   ,,
     16. Finani Ep.   ,,   ,,
     17. Patricii Archiep. dup. added in red.
Ap. 18. Laceriani Ep. C. dup. fest. per co. Dublin. added in red.
May   7. Joh. de beuerlaco added in black.
     13. Sythe V. non mart. added in red.
     16. Brandani Abb. added in red.
June 3. Keuinii Abb. added in black.
      7. Columbe Abb. dup. fest. per co. Dublinie added in red.
     10. Transl. S. patricii added in red.
July 3. Visit. B.V.M. added in red.
     13. S. Henrici Imperatoris et conf. added in black.
Aug. 25. S. Michee Archiep. primatis hibernie ix lect. added in red.
Sept. 6. S. Macurlini Ep. ? added, in red.
Oct. 17. S. Etheldrede V. non M. added in red.
     19. S. Frideswide V. added in red.
     26. Med. lect. de S. Joh. beuerlaco cum Resp. de iiᵒ
          Nocturno added in black.

Nov. 3. S. Wenefride V.M. ix lect. added in black.
      14. Transl. S. Erkenwaldi Ep. C. dup. fest. ap. london.
            added in red.
Dec. 4. S. Osmundi Ep. C. Inuit. dup. ix lect. added in black.
      29. S. Thomas of Canterbury erased.

There are handsome borders and decorative initials to each division, principal feast and nocturne of the Psalter.

I. 3. 12   C. M. A. 126

65. HOROLOGIUM SAPIENTIAE ETC.

Vellum, $8\frac{1}{8} \times 5\frac{1}{2}$, ff. 191 + 3, 36 lines to a page. Cent. xv, clearly written.

From Kirkham Priory, Yorks., as appears by the matter on the flyleaves.

Given by Tho. Bywater to the College.

Collation: 3 flyleaves (2 + 1). 1^{12}–16^{12} (wants 12).

On the flyleaf:

Liber Roberti *Fowberii* (written over erasure) quem comparauit Ebor. tercio die mensis maii a.d. mill. quadringentesimo septuag. octauo. Precium xii*s*. Osanna.

Then a series of documents about the founder of Kirkham Priory.

1. Dominus Walterus Espek miles strenuus decorus in etate iuuenili duxit uxorem quandam nomine Adelinam
    —fundans tria monasteria prout inferius patebit.
2. Anno ab incarn. domini m^{mo} c^{mo} xxii sancte trinitatis ecclesia in kirkham fundata est etc.
    —ad uitam migrauit eternam. Amen.
3. Predictus autem Walterus Espeke fundauit tria monasteria
    —iacens ibidem in sua ecclesia humatus vij idus marcii a.d. M.C. liiii cuius anime propicietur deus. Amen.
4. Verses (22). Pandere progeniem de Ros cupiens seriatim
                 Le spek Walterum scribere uolo prius
                         ...
            M. simul et C. ter x et sex hiis sociatis
            Transiit autumpno vir bonus ille deo.
5. Birth of William filius d. Will. de Ros domini de hamelake ex d. matilda filie (!) d. Joh. de Wallibus (1291, in Cathedra S. Petri).
    The same note repeated.
    Two tables of contents, one of cent. xv.

Contents:

I. 3. 13. Bound with I. 2. 15.

I. 3. 14   C. M. A. 29

66. LYNDWOOD ETC.

Paper and vellum, $7\frac{7}{8} \times 5\frac{1}{2}$, two volumes. I. Paper. Cent. xv
late, 32 lines to a page. II. Vellum, double columns of 48 lines.
Cent. xiii, in a beautiful small hand.
Given by Tho. Leigh.
Collation: 3 flyleaves. I. 1^{12} 2^{12} (wants 1)–5^{12}, ff. 59. II. 1^{12}
(wants 1)–8^{12}, ff. 96 | 3 flyleaves.

Contents :

I.   Constitutiones prouinciales Anglie .   .   .   .   .   .   f.   1
    De summa trinitate et fide catholica.
    Ignorancia sacerdotum et cetera.   Ne quis per ignoranciam
    se excuset.
    Ends f. 55 with a constitution of Winchelsea beginning
    Abiuraciones autem fornicariarum.
    Table   .   .   .   . 55 *b*
    Ends f. 59 *a*: Expl. tabula Constit. prouincialium, 59 *b* blank.
II. Raymundi summa confessorum   1
    Distinguitur hoc opus in tres particulas.
    Capitula of Part I.
    Text.   Quoniam inter crimina ecclesiastica.
    Ends f. 95 *a*: Venite benedicti patres mei etc.
    Finito libro *sit laus* et gloria *christo.*
    hic liber *est scriptus* qui scripsit *sit bene* dictus.
    Italicised words in red : erasure follows.
    On the flyleaves, a formula, some receipts (one in English) and
    verses, and the name William James (xvi).

I. 3. 15

67. BIBLIA.

Vellum, $7\frac{5}{8} \times 5\frac{1}{2}$, ff. 522, double columns of 46 lines.   Cent. xiii,
in an excellent hand.
Given by Tho. Leigh.   The name Henricus Gocheus and
praec. 11*s*. 6*d*. on f. 1.   On the page after the Interpretationes is
written Scti Dunstani in oriente London. (xvi), and on the last
page Rychard Lynccon (xv, xvi).

At the end of the Apocalypse is an erased inscription.
Collation: 1^{12} (wants 4)–4^{12} 5^{10} 6^{12} 7^{10} 8^{10} 9^{12}–22^{12} (wants 10) 23^{12}–29^{12} (wants 11) 30^{12}–38^{12} (wants 11, 12) 39^{14} (wants 1, 2) 40^{16} (+ 1) 41^{12}–44^{12}.

Contents:

Prologues of Jerome.   *a.* Frater Ambrosi.
                       b. Desiderii mei.
Genesis (1st leaf gone) to 2 Par. (without Prayer of Manasses).
Ezra, Nehemiah, 2 Esdras (= 1 Esdras of Apocr.).
Tobit—Job, followed by Hic testatur iob de resurrectione.
  Iob quoque exemplar patientie—spes mea in sinu meo.
Origo prophetie psalmorum. Dauid filius Iesse.
  Psalterium Rome dudum positus.
Psalter Gallican. Ps. cli.
Prov. Ecclus. (ch. lii is oratio Salomonis): a leaf gone in Wisdom.
Isa.—Malachi, 1st leaf of Daniel gone.
1, 2 Maccabees.
Evv., Paul. Epp. (omit. Col. iii—2 Tim. iii).
Acts (ending per quem incipiet totus mundus iudicari).
Cath. Epp. with the reading deglutiens mortem etc. in 1 Pet. iii.
Apoc.
Interpretationes nominum in another hand. Aaz—Zuzim.
With curious outline grotesques on the lower margins: ending
  f. 519 *b.*
Pencil notes on 520–522.

Historiated initials: gold grounds: colours rather pale: decent English work.

Prologue. Man writing at desk. *Gen.* Gone.
Exod. Moses and Aaron walk to *R.* followed by the people.
Lev. Moses horned speaks to half-length figure in building on *R.*
Num. Similar. Moses is seated. *Deut.* Gone.
Jos. leads the people to *R.*
Jud. Nimbed figure on *L.* Red river, people on *R.*
Ruth. Boaz above. Ruth with sheaf below.
1 *Reg.* Hannah delivers Samuel to Eli on *R.*
2 *Reg.* David seated. Amalekite with crown kneeling.
3 *Reg.* David in bed. Abishag rubs his feet.
4 *Reg.* Ahaziah in bed, three men by him.
1 *Par.* Group of seated figures.
2 *Par.* Solomon seated with crown and sceptre.
Ezra. Large figure of Ezra in cap.
Neh. Seated writing. 2 *Esdr.* Decorative.
Tobit. Seated blind, Anna on *R.* Tobias and Raphael on *R.*
Judith. Beheads Holofernes. Maid on *L.*
Esther. Below, touches sceptre of Ahasuerus above.

Job. Nude, reclines. Three friends on *R.*

Psalms. Beatus vir. Christ above half-length with orb. David with harp below.
Dominus illuminatio. Samuel anoints David.
Dixi custodiam. David sits with hand to mouth.
Dixit insipiens. Man seated cross-legged, hawk on hand.
Salvum. Christ half-length with orb. David in water below.
Exultate. David plays on bells.
Cantate. David plays dulcimer.
Dixit Dominus. The Father and Son seated.

Prov. Eccl. Solomon with scroll.

Cant. Crowned figures, one with cross, embrace.

Wisd. Solomon with sword and scales.

Ecclus. As Prov.

Isaiah. With scroll. *Jeremiah.* At gate of city. *Baruch.* With scroll.

Ezekiel. On *R.* in cloud heads of Christ and the 4 beasts. *Daniel.* Gone.

Hosea. Embraces Gomer. *Joel.* Gone. *Amos.* With scroll and sheep.

Obadiah. With scroll. *Jonah.* Emerges from fish: Nineveh above.

Micah. With scroll. *Nahum.* City on *R.*

Habakkuk to *Malachi.* Single figures with scrolls.

1 *Macc.* Horsemen on *L.* Angel on *R.* (Heliodorus?)

2 *Macc.* Jews on *L.* Messenger on *R.* with scroll.

Matthew. On *L.* Jesse on *R.* sleeping. Virgin and Child above.

Mark. Lion on medallion above him. *Luke.* Writing: ox above desk.

John. Eagle above him in medallion.

Rom.—Phil. Paul seated, addresses people on *R.*

Tit.—Philem. Paul conversing with a single man.

Heb. Paul addresses Jews.

Acts. Apostles in two groups.

James. Single figure. 1 *Peter.* Peter as bishop seated with cross-staff.

2 *Peter.* Peter seated bareheaded.

1–3 *John.* John seated. *Jude.* Single figure.

Apoc. John writing.

I. 3. 16

68. POEMS ETC.

Paper, 8 × 6, ff. circ. 160. Cent. xvii, several volumes.
A list of contents in Dr Farmer's hand.

Contents:

I.   1.   Elisaeis Apotheosis poetica sive de florentissimo imperio et
          rebus gestis......Elizabethae.
          Poematis in duodecim libros tribuendi liber primus.
          Authore Gul. Alabastro Cantabr. Colleg. Trin.

Dedication to Elizabeth in prose. Elegiacs follow.
Text begins : Virgineum mundi decus augustamque
Britannae.

II. 2. Poems by Dr Donne, viz. Praise of middle age . . p. 2
Donnes Prayse of an Old woman.
His Parting wth his M^{rs}.
To his M^{rs}. I wonder (by my troth) what thou and I.
A Sonnet. Send home my long strayd eys to me.
Mummy.
A Song. When I dyed last.
    The haire a forest is of ambushes.
Discovered by a Perfume.
Selecta. In a garden. His Curse. A diet for Love.
As the sweet sweat of Roses in a still.

    3. The Inner Temple Masque. Jan. 13, 1614. Written by
        W. Browne (author of Brittannia's Pastorals) . . 8

III. 4. Pseudo Magia, Authore M^{ro} Mewe Cant. Col. Eman. . 17
        Mr Mewe was afterwards rector of Eastington (Glouc^s.).

IV. 5. Paria, Authore Thoma Vincent, Trin. Coll. Soc. Cant. . 49
        (Acta coram Sereniss. Rege Carolo. Mar. 3, 1627. Ab
        hora undecima ad quintam.)

V. 6. Parthenia. Comoedia pastoralis.

VI.   Miscellaneous Poems.

    1. The Harte. Whilome diuided from ye maine lande stoode

        Whom it arisinge from the sea deterres.
    Georgɪvs ᴅvx Bvckɪnghaмɪe (chronogram on 1628).
        Thy numerous name with thy yeare doth agree
        But 29 heauen grant thou ne're maist see.

    2. On his Mrs Picture. Such clowdes and shadowes may
        content the minde.
    3. Now westward Sol had spent the richest beames.
    4. When first I sawe thee thou didst sweetly playe.
    5. Rare creature let me speake wthout offence.
    6. Poems on the death of Queen Elizabeth. *a.* By Ed.
        Kellet, Regal. *b.* The early houres. *c.* By Th. Cecill,
        Joh. *d.* By F. Bowle, Trin.
    7. Sir R. Bacon. The world's a buble.
    8. John to Jeane. Tell me sweete Jugge.
    9. Upon a blemish in a Lady's eye.
  10. Upon a woman and her childe haueinge each of y^m but
       one eye.
  11. In Nuptias Geo. Goringe. When I my serious thoughts
       had set.
  12. Caryes Rapture. I will enioye yee now my Celia come.
  13. Upon o^r Ladyes daye, 2 dayes before o^r Soueraignes.
  14. To a beautifull Lady perswasions to Love. Think not
       'cause men do flatteringe saye.

15. The Epicures paradoxe.   No worldlinge noe 'tis not thye
    golde.
16. Twixt hope and feare the best affection sits.
17. A faire yet hard M^{rs}: Nowe y^t ye winters gone.
18. To a gentlewoman y^t desired a H^{rs} helpe to make her faire.
    ffaire one! y' have posed me and my skill: you craue.
19. An old dittye of Sr Philip Sidneyes.
    Philoclea and Pamela sweete.

I. 3. 17   C. M. A. 12

69. JOHN OF ARDERN.

Paper, 8¼ × 5¾, ff. 210, 29 lines to a page.   Cent. xv, clearly
written, with curious drawings.   Stamped leather binding of
cent. xvi.

Collegio Emanuelis sacrum posuit Humfredus Moseley armiger
et Sociorum Commensalis 1649.

Collation: 1^{16} (15, 16 canc.) 2^{12}–16^{12} 17^6 18^4 19^2 20$^?$ (four left,
last stuck to cover).

Contents :

Circle marked with names of winds, quarters of globe etc.   .   f.   1 b
Collection of receipts in English, probably all by John Ardern of
    Newark: illustrated with rough coloured drawings of herbs,
    instruments and patients: not to be described in detail.
It begins
This is a mirrour of bloodletynge in þe weche þey þ^t wolen
    beholden it diligently.
On f. iii *b* are names of herbs in French: on iii *a* a receipt for
    Greek fire in French.
At f. 191 is a table of contents ending
    Expl. tabula libri Sirurgice Mag. Joh. Arderne de Newerk.
A Receipt in another hand follows, ff. 199, 200 blank.
Further receipts in two good hands   201
Beginning of alphabetical table   .   .   .   .   208 *b*

I. 3. 18   C. M. A. 39

70. ASTRONOMICA ETC.

Paper, 8 × 5¾, ff. 150 + 2, mostly 45 lines to a page.   Cent. xv,
closely written with some good drawings.

1667. Ex dono Tho. Leigh S. Theol. Bacc. Coll. Emman. nuper Socii.

Collation: 1 flyleaf. 1⁸ (wants 1)–19⁸ (wants 5): 1 flyleaf.

On the flyleaf: Master harssedecon (Archdeacon : xv).

Nota quod nomina trium regum sunt hec ut scribit magister in historia scolastica. Hebraice Appelius Amerus Damascus. Grece Galgalat Malgaleb Serachin. Latine Jaspar Balthesar Melchior.

Note that John Baptist was born anno mundi 5198 etc.

On f. 2 :

Dunstapl*us* conscripsit hunc librum.

Astronomical note and table of contents.

Contents :

Nomina planetarum et aspectus lune ad eos   .   .   . f. 63 *b*

Tract. de cogitacione et intencione.   Messahallac .   .   .   64

Interpretacio quam puto esse messeallath   .   .   .   .   64 *b*

Dorotheus de re occulta   65

Tract in 8 chapters of Willelmus Anglicus on astrology and
medicine   .   .   .   .   66 *b*

Ne uel ignorancie uel pocius inuidie redarguat mi germane qui
quando apud marsilium aliquantulum studuisti.

Liber Iergis de significacionibus 7 planetarum in 12 domibus .   69

Dixit iergis. Saturnus cum fuerit.

Tract. haly de proprietatibus lune in qualibet domo   .   .   71

Luna cum fuerit in prima domo.

Haly de tempore sec. quemlibet planetam in quolibet signo   72

Saturnus in ariete sub radiis.   f. 73 *a* blank.

Judicium Messehalla super questiones cuiusdam ducis prout
sequitur   73

Interrogacio cuiusdam ducis quam proposuit rex affrice.

75 *b*—78 *a* blank.

Extractum ex 5° (?) cap. de Exafranon.

7. Inc. breuiloquium mag. bartholomei nacione permensis bononie
compilatum et confirmatum per prudentes uiros de fructis
tocius astronomie ad preces domini Thedisii de fusco a° 1286°   80

Prol. Scribit philosophus in primo libro methaphisice.

Text. Gloriosus et eternus deus   81

Ends f. 118 *b* (on *Vexillum*): sui aspectus in celo.

Expl. breuiloq.—a° 1286°. quod Dunstaple Deo gracias.

In this tract are drawings of constellations in medallions for the
most part, in good shaded pen and ink, with the stars
marked in red, beginning at f. 89 *b*, as follows:

Aries. Taurus. Gemini (marked as Castor and Pollux, winged,
in cloaks, Pollux with harp). Cancer. Leo. Virgo winged
with sheaf. Libra held by man in cap. Scorpius. Sagittarius,
centaur with body of horse and body of lion on its back,
shooting to *L*. Capricorn ending in cornucopiae. Aquarius,
bearded man pouring out urn. Pisces.

Ursa major and minor with Draco (a serpent).

Draco, winged dragon on rocks.

Hercules, nude with sword and lion's skin, attacks serpent in
tree on *L*.

Corona, circle of stars.

Serpentarius (Ophiuchus), nude, holds snake and stands on
Scorpius.

Boetes, in cap and tunic, holds sickle and spear.

"Agitator," man with spear and two small beasts on his *L.*
hand standing in a waggon drawn by 3 horses.

Cepheus (Orion?) full face, hands raised, sword belt and sword.

Cassiopoeia seated full face, hands raised, four swords behind
her, two horizontal, two vertical.

Pegasus, winged horse.

Andromeda, bearded, full face, hands raised.

Perseus, cloak and shield, Gorgon's head (bearded), raised sword.

Triangulus.

Gallina siue clocha. Seven maidens, four behind, three in front. Lyra.

Cygnus. Vultur volans (on arrow). Vultur cadens pierced by a man: arrow below.

Cetus, nude man below, rock and city above. Eridianus, man sits playing dulcimer.

Delphinus: rock and city above. Orion in plate armour: shield and raised sword.

Canis. Lepus. Nauis. Astronochus, a female centaur. Demon meridianus: two figures seated, the one on *R*. holds up an elliptical ring. No stars marked.

Piscis magnus et minor. Two fishes in water; the lower one larger, on its back.

Putheus, a group of demons surrounding a huge face in *C*.

Centaurus, centaur walking to *R*. carrying hare and bear (?), from his *R*. hand hangs a censer.

Ydra, snake with crow and pitcher on back approaching tree on *L*. Cyon (Procyon), dog. Equus secundus, winged horse. Tarabellum, an auger. Vexillum, a banner.

f. 119 blank.

8. Inc. Ciromantia. Secantur sciencie inter se . . . . f. 120
—Et sic est finis artis cyromancie, deo gracias. Expl. hic Cyrom. Deo sit honor laus et gloria quod Dunst.

9. De Chiromantia. Cum tractare (?) vel unde Cyromantia   . 129
A further extract on the same. Si sub linea vite. 133, 134 *a* blank   132

10. Inc. phizo(no)mia aristotelis. Inter ceteras sciencias . . 134 *b*
—declina semper ad melius. Expl. phizzonomia quod Dunst.
Two astronomical notes 135 *b*.

11. Inc. tract. de modo componendi almanach. In composicione almanach sic procede 136
Miscell. notes 136 *b*.

12. Inc. lib. auenesre israelite de mundo s. de reuolucione annorum mundi s. de reuol. annorum seculi . . . . . 137 *b*
Tractatus auenesre de planetarum coniunccionibus
—semper intendas. Expl. lib. de mundo et seculo completus die Jouis post fest. S. barnabe Ap. sub ascendente scorpionis a. d. 1292° in perside (?) translatus autem a mag. Henr. dicto bate de machelia de hebreo in latinum. d. g. quod Dunst.
Notes f. 144.
Inc. pronosticaciones de eclipsi uniuersali lune et de coniunccionibus 3 planetarum superiorum que apparuerunt a. d. 1345 in marcio et complete fuerunt iste pronost. 24 die predicti mensis anni predicti . . . . . . 144 *b*

E. C. C.   5

De coniunccione Saturni et Jouis a° 1345 (per M. Jo. Asshenden)   f. 145 *b*
Notes, some from Albumazar.
Messehalla de mercibus (?)   .   .   .   .   147 *b*
Attende ergo ad ea que dicam
  —utile uenditori.
Notes and diagrams.
Liber Albumasar de coniunccionibus (diagrams and notes)   .   151 *b*
ff. 153–157 *a* blank: scribbles of Richard Stonnerd Kingele in
  County of Surrey.
Notes and receipts, some in English (on Apothecaries' signs)   .   157 *b*
Last flyleaf: notes and receipts: in one "hanc medicinam
  expertus fuit ultimo anno M. Joh. Wendouere de nome in
  quodam habente duo ulcera."

I. 3. 19
71.

Paper, $7\frac{1}{2} \times 5\frac{3}{4}$, ff. circ. 100 written, more than half the volume
blank.   Cent. xvii.

Richardus Tertius.

(By Dr T. Legge (1536–1607) Master of Caius College.)
Dramatis Personae, and names of the actors.

D. Shephard, Elizabetha Regina etc.
Chapman.   Argumentum primae actionis.
Text.   *Eliz.* quicunque laetus credulus rebus nimis.

Printed by B. Field in 1844 for the Shakespeare Society.
Another MS. is at Gonville and Caius College (no. 125).
At the other end :

Copies of addresses and letters of the University:
  1. To the Chancellor.   8 Kal. Dec. 1627.
  2.   „   13 Kal. Dec. 1621.
  3. To Sam. Harsnett Abp designate of York, 18 Nov. 1628.
  4. To Sir Francis Cottington, 1628.
  5. To Laud, Bp of London.
  6. Goodwin, Fellow of Trinity College, to (Marc. Ant. de Dominis)
      Abp of Spalatro, in St Mary's Church.

I. 3. 20
72.   HORAE.

Vellum, $8\frac{1}{4} \times 5\frac{3}{4}$, ff. 117, 14 lines to a page.   Cent. xv early, in
bold English hand with fine ornaments in rough style.

In several places is the name Elizabeth Plunket (Plonket) badly written, perhaps by a child.

Collation: 1⁸⁷ (wants 1–6) 2⁸ 3⁶ 4⁶ 5⁸–7⁸ 8⁶–10⁶ 11⁸ 12⁸ (wants 8) 13⁸ (+ 1) 14⁸ 15⁸ 16⁶ (+ 4*) 17⁸ (wants 7, 8): these are the first six leaves of quire 1.

Contents:

  ff. 89–117 should precede f. 1.
The Memoriae are written on one side of the leaf only.
There is no means of settling the provenance that I can detect. The use is of Sarum. Litany and Memoriae are not otherwise distinctive.
The ornament consists wholly of borders and decorative initials.

I. 3. 21

73. ENCHIRIDION AUGUSTINI, ETC.

Vellum, 7¾ × 5¾, ff. 68 + 5, 27 lines to a page.   Cent. xii early, in a fine hand.   2 fo. iam meruit.

Given by Thomas Comber (?).   At the end is a Greek note signed by him.

An erasure on the flyleaf.

Stamped leather binding of cent. xvi: two clasps.

Collation: 1 flyleaf.   1⁸–5⁸ 6⁶ 7⁸–9⁸ (7, 8 canc.): b⁴.

Contents:

A table on flyleaf, headed
  Hec in isto uolumine continentur.
1. Title in red capitals. Inc. Enchiridion Augustini quem scripsit ad Laurentinium.

Dici non potest (XL. 231) . . . . . . f. 1
  —conscripsi. Expl. ench. Aug. quem scripsit ad
   Laurentium.

2. In another hand
  Sermo S. Augustini qualiter homo factus est ad Imaginem et
   similitudinem Dei.
    Tanta dignitas (XL. 1213) 46
    —in secundo reformauit. Amen.

3. In the former hand
  Inc. Liber S. Ambrosii Ep. de bono mortis (XIV. 539) . 47
   Quoniam superiori libro
    —in sec. sec. Amen.

A large circular erasure 67 b: f. 68 blank, except for note by
Comber.

Flyleaves: four leaves (the first page in double column) in a
curious ugly hand, with sermons or other matter on the
passion.

  Hodie sanctus sanctorum dominus cui a patre cum iura-
  mento dictum est tu es sacerdos etc.

Followed by a short note in another hand.

I. 3. 22   C. M. A. 40

74. BREVILOQUIUM PAUPERIS.

Vellum, 8⅛ × 6, ff. 115, 28 lines to a page.   Cent. xv, well
written.

Given by Tho. Leigh.   2 fo. verum eciam.
Collation: 1⁸–14⁸ 15⁴ (4 canc.).

Contents:

  Inc. breuiloquium pauperis in sacra scriptura fratris Bonaventure.
   Flecto genua mea ad patrem.
  In seven parts, ending f. 114 b: donec intrem in gaudium dei mei.
  Qui est trinus et unus deus benedictus in sec. sec. Amen.
   Expl. breuiloquium pauperis in sacra scriptura ffratris Bona-
   uenture ordinis minorum et cardinalis Albanensis.
  f. 115 blank.

I. 3. 23   C. M. A. 134

75.

Paper, 7⅝ × 5¾, ff. 43, 17 lines to a page.   Cent. xvii.
Given by Joshua Barnes in 170½.

A good binding, with large central stamp of the Royal arms, with crown and supporters, and angle-stamps of thistles.

Statutes of the Order of the Garter as reformed by Henry VIII. In English. Ends with an enactment of 13 Elizabeth touching precedence of knights.

At the end this note in Barnes's hand :

This Book was found among certaine others wch belonged to King James and after his Death came into the hands of Mr Peck, Prebend of Westminster.

I. 3. 24   C. M. A. 75

76. Life of Sir T. More.

Paper, 8⅛ × 6¼, ff. 57 + 12 + 46 written.   Cent. xvi, for the most part in a beautifully neat hand.

Vellum wrapper.   Note in the cover by Dr Farmer attributing the text to Nicholas Harpsfield.

Also this note:

This booke was founde by Rich: Topclyff in Mr Thomas Moare(s) Studdye emongs other bookes at Greenstreet Mr Wayfarers hovse when Mr Moare was apprehended the XIIIth of Aprill 1582.

Contents:

Life of Sir Thomas More.
    Dedication to Will. Roper, signed N. H. L. D.
    Text ends f. 57: longe preserue the Realme. Amen.
    Speeches of More on the Act of Supremacy. ff. 12.
    More's Confession of belief. ff. 44.
    Certaine notes of Doctor Hardius death noted in a sermon made at his monthes minde ye XIIIIth of October 1573 in Antwerpe vppon these words *Eamus et nos et moriamur cum eo.* ff. 2.

Another MS. of this Life is in MS. Harley 6253.

I. 3. 25

77.

Paper, 7⅞ × 5¾, two volumes.

Contents:

I.   Κατάργησις Scandali contra Andreae Laurentii dogmata de Strumis (a) Regibus anglorum non curandis.
    Cui annexa est altera quaestio
                An amor sit morbus.

Five stanzas (four-lined) of French verse.   Au Lecteur.
Or France à quel propos deviens tu si fascheuse?
Dedication by Richard Spicer to Ludovicus Leviniae Dux,
Richmundiae et Darliae Comiti etc.
Text occupying 17 ff.

II. Documents connected with Lichfield Diocese.   Cent. xvi.
Pensiones debite sol. ecclesie Cathed. Lich(feld).
The parishes are set out in alphabetical order, and copies of
old grants etc. given for each. ff. 12.
Pensiones solut. a. d. 1560 vel solui de(bentes) ex libro mei
Walkeri communarii 4° eod. anno. ff. 2.
Statement on the foundation of Lichfield.   Copies of Papal
documents etc. (in two hands). ff. 4.
2 ff. with a list of Obits very badly written, the reverse way.

I. 3. 26
78. FRANCIAS BARNESII.

Paper, 8 × 5⅞, pp. 197 written.   Cent. xvii, in a clear hand.
Probably given by Joshua Barnes.
Notes in his hand are in the cover and on the flyleaves.

Franciados libri I—VII.
An Epic poem in Latin on the French wars of Edward III, by Joshua Barnes.
Arguments are prefixed.   The text begins f. 2:
Illo ego qui Graeco diuinum carmen ab ore.
The text is on one side of the leaf only.   The hand changes a good deal: there are
various notes by Barnes.   At the end:
Franciados Lib. VIII correctior in codice minutulo pergamena involuto extat.
circa 700 versus.

I. 3. 27
79.

Paper, 8 × 6, and 7½ × 5¾, ff. 18 and 14.   Two volumes: neatly
written in double columns, sideways on the page.   Cent. xvii.
Given by the author, Joshua Barnes.

I. Dedication by Barnes (?) to John Bretton, Master.   28 Mar.
1673.
Title. Sacra Biblia Compendiosa sive Μεταφράσεις quaedam
ex utroque Testamento selectae.   Liber Tertius.
Dedication to John Bretton.

Paraphrases in Greek hexameters of the Song of Moses,
Sermon on the Mount, etc., followed by a few "Epigrams"
in various metres addressed to members of Emmanuel and
other Colleges.

II. Παλίζωος "Ομηρος sive Poemation de Vatum Patre et Principe
Homero.

Dedicated by Barnes to Jac. Duport, Master of Magdalene,
Dean of Peterborough, etc.

In Homeric hexameters (188), followed by some "Epigrams"
of Barnes's.

The date 1673 is at the end.

I. 3. 28

80.

Paper, 7⅞ × 6¼, ff. 59 written, circ. 30 blank, some loose papers (3)
in the volume. Cent. xvi, for the most part well written.
Vellum wrapper.

The coppie of a letter written by a Mr of Arts in Cambridge to his
freinde in London concerninge some talke passed of late betweene
worshipfull and graue menn. Aboute the present state and some
proceedings of the Earle of Leicester and his freindes in England.

Epistle dedicatorie to Mr G. M. in Gratious streete London.

Text ends f. 54 b: Finis, L. D.

Meditation on Job xxviii, signed L. Daneidis . . . . f. 55
In a later hand. Notes about the Earls of Essex . . . 55 b
Sir John Harrington's Epigram on Mary Queen of Scots etc.
Pedigrees of the Earls of Derby and Essex.
Earl of Essex's "complaint of a sinnere."
    Oh heuenly god O father dear cast downe thy tender eye.

A loose paper with Latin verses addressed to Rob. Dudley Earl
of Leicester by Walter Haddon, Vtenhuius and D. Wilson.

Two original letters.

1. Endorsed. To his lovinge Awnte Mistres Mary Draycott yeve thes at
Manyneston (?).

Letter of condolence (Dublin 13 Sept. (?) 1576) signed Rob. Bisse, Margret Bisse,
Cicely Fagan.

A note on the edge says, This Letter sheeth the death of Olfer (?) Draycott to be
in a. 1576.

2. Endorsed. To his welbeloved frend Mrs Alies Draycot these geve.

Headed with mottoes. Scopus vitae Christus etc.

Address in English verse accompanying a book.

    As I my werie limmes reposde to take my wontede rest.

Ends, your assured to vse YF.

I. 3. 29

81. Biblia.

Vellum, 7⅝ × 5⅛, ff. 464, double columns of 48 lines. Cent. xiii, in a very good small hand. 2 fo. Ihesum qui.
Old binding skin formerly red over boards: clasps gone.
Covers lined with bits of a xivth (?) cent. Canon Law MS.
Collation: 1^{14} 2^{14} 3^{16}–10^{16} 11^{16} (one canc.) 12^{16}-25^{16} 26^4 | 27^{12} 28^{10} 29^{12}-31^{12} 32^8 (wants 8).

Contents:

> Genesis—2 Chron. (Prayer of Manasses follows without a break) with the usual prologues.
> Ezra, Nehemiah, Tobit, Judith, Hester, Job.
> Proverbs—Ecclus.
> Isa.—Malachi.
> 1, 2 Maccabees.
> Evv., Act., Paul. Epp., Cath. Epp., Apoc.
> Interpretationes nominum (Aaz—Zuzim) in another hand.
> List of the books of O.T. and of the Cantica in a third hand.

The following pictured initials occur:

Prol. Monk writing scroll at desk.
Gen. Long initial. Ground half blue, half red, with patterns. Eight medallions (square in quatrefoil) on gold ground. The seven days of Creation, and the Crucifixion with the Virgin and John. Delicate bright colour.
Exod. Miriam (or Pharaoh's daughter) raising Moses in ark out of water.
Lev. Two men converse. *Num.* Moses seated between two men.
Deut. Moses addresses two vertical lines of heads on *R.* (ten in all).
Jos. Moses (?) speaks to Joshua. *Jud.* Joshua (?) addresses four men. *Ruth.* Decorative.
1 *Reg.* Hannah, Elkanah (turning to her) and Peninnah (children in lap) seated on a bench.
2, 3, 4 *Reg.* Decorative. 1 *Par.* Solomon seated. Temple on *R.* 2 *Par.* 1, 2 *Esdr.* Decorative.
Tob. Tobit sleeping. *Judith.* Beheads Holofernes armed sitting up in bed.
Esther. Decorative. *Job.* Seated, nude. Devil on *R.*
Prov. Solomon seated. Three heads on *R.*
Eccl., *Cant.* Decorative. *Sap.* Solomon standing, 4 heads on *R.* *Ecclus.* Solomon seated. Rehoboam seated on *R.*
Isaiah. Stands nude, bound. Two men saw him asunder (upwards).
Jeremiah. On *L.* Christ on *R.* A pot in air in *C.* *Lam.* Jeremiah seated, hand to head.
Baruch. Decorative. *Ezekiel.* Reclining, rayed cloud above. *Daniel.* Four

heads on *L.* Tower on *R.* Heads of Daniel and two lions seen in it.   *Hosea.*
Embraces Gomer.
Joel. Two groups of men, edge of coloured sphere above.   *Amos.* In cap and
tunic gathers fruit.
Obadiah. Decorative.   *Jonah.* Nude, rides on whale.   *Micah.* A man in
tunic on *L.* smites him with a rod on the face.   *Nahum.* Two broken horseless
chariots.   *Habakkuk.* The Child Christ in manger.   Ass and ox at head and feet.
Zeph. Water with fishes flows from porch on *R.*
Hagg., Zech. Decorative.   *Malachi.* Angel on *L.*   Man in porch on *R.* turns away.
1 *Macc.* Three mailed men in tower on elephant's back.   Eleazar Maccabaeus below.
2 *Macc.* A knight in square casque with lance in rest riding to *R.*
Matt. Angel with scroll.   *Marc.* Decorative, winged lion at bottom.   *Luc.* Winged
beast, dark blue, more like lion than ox.   *Joh.* Decorative, with bust of John.
Acts. Two groups of men.   Head of Dove in *C.* above.
Rom. Paul crouching on ground.   1 *Cor.* Addressing three men.   2 *Cor.* Decorative.
Gal. Paul standing.   *Eph.* Decorative.   *Phil.* Paul holds sword under his
chin.   *Col.* Seated, looking up.   1 *Thess.* Writing.   2 *Thess.* Kneeling.   1 *Tim.*
Writing.   2 *Tim.* Reading.   *Titus.* Writing.   *Philem.* With open book,
man on *R.*   *Heb.* Decorative.
James. Decorative.   1 *Pet.* Peter writing.   2 *Pet.* Decorative.   1 *Joh.*
John standing.   2, 3 *John, Jude.* Decorative.
Apoc. Christ with book blessing.
These initials are of excellent execution: the grounds are mostly blue or brown.

I. 4. 1, 2   Printed Bible.

I. 4. 3

82. BIBLIA.

Vellum (uterine), 6½ × 4½, ff. 628, double columns of 45 lines.
Cent. xiii (middle) in a beautiful regular hand.   Fine ornaments.
2 fo. quam stultitia.

On f. 256 is the name or word Yottyn.

Collation: 1²⁰ (wants 1) 2²⁴–8²⁴ 9²⁰ 10²⁴ 11²⁴ (two canc.) 12¹⁶ 13¹⁴
(wants 14) | 14²⁴–27²⁴ 28⁴ 29⁶.

Contents:

> Jerome's Prologues: Frater Ambrosius.
> > Desiderii mei.
>
> Genesis—2 Chronicles.   Prayer of Manasses follows 2 Chron.
> without a break.
> Ezra, Nehemiah, 1 Esdras of Apocrypha (called here Esdre II.).
> Tobit, Judith, Esther, Job.
> Psalter (Gallican).
> Proverbs—Ecclus.

Isaiah—Malachi.

1, 2 Maccabees.

Evv., Paul. Epp., Acts, Cath. Epp., Apoc., ending
  Explicit bibliotheca.

Interpretationes nominum. 'Aaz—Zuzim.

Expl. interpretationes. f. 622 (blank) has an old pencil note
  Ypof'ta (? Apocrypha) esdre continet 30...Capitula.
  In a xvth cent. hand. Table of Epistles and Gospels . . f. 623
  The feasts of SS. Alban, Leger, Edmund, Hugo are noted.

The figured subjects are as follows :

1. *Prologue.* Monk writing at desk. This page is bordered.

2. *Gen.* Initial containing seven small elliptical miniatures of the days of Creation
(the seventh day at the top), and also of the Fall and Crucifixion. All on gold ground.
At bottom a peacock.

3. *Exodus.* Moses horned with rod and tables.

4. 1 *Chron.* Seated figure.

5. *Tobit.* Seated with cap and staff.

6. *Judith.* With sword and head of Holofernes.

7. *Job.* Seated nude on dunghill.

8. *Prov.* Solomon seated crowned on *R*. Rehoboam nude seated on *L*. Centaur
above.

9. *Ecclus.* Crowned figure with sceptre pointing upward.

The rest are all decorative and in excellent style.

I. 4. 4   C. M. A. 79
83.

Vellum, 6⅝ × 5, ff. 215, 19 lines to a page. Cent. xii late, in a
beautiful round hand.   2 fo. dem suam habet.

Collation : 1⁸ 2⁶ (5, 6 canc.) 3¹²–6¹² 7¹⁴ 8¹²–15¹² 16⁸ 17⁸ (wants 1)
18¹⁴ 19¹² 20⁶ (5, 6 canc.).

Contents :

A miscellaneous collection chiefly of a series of tracts without
  authors' names on the seven deadly sins, intended for the use
  of persons confessing, and for confessors.

1. Diffinitio anime. Anima ut uult aristoteles in secundo de anima f. 1
   Various extracts on the functions of the soul, on the imagination,
   on dreams.
   ff. 11, 12 blank.

2. Twenty-six questions on the sentences 13
   Secundo libro sentent. D. xxi capitulo Porro.
     Dicitur quod due sunt species temptationis.
   The initial in blue, light brown and green is exceedingly pretty
   and unusual : another by the same hand is on f. 87.

Responsiones magistri ad premissas questiones . . . f. 15
    Reuerendo patri suo semper in Christo et cum reuerentia
    diligendo domino Benedicto priori de Ramesya suus in
    Christo semper filius sospitatem etc.

3. Contra pudorem confitendi 34
4. De duobus generibus peccatorum generalissimis . . . 37
    Quedam dicuntur spiritualia.
5. From f. 37 *b* onwards there is a series of tracts on the seven
    sins and the modes of confessing them: also on the senses
    and Commandments.
    The ninth of these f. 119 *b* is
        Item de uiciis in gallico ideomate.
    Noted by M. Paul Meyer (*MSS. Français de Cambridge*,
    Trinity Coll. p. 41, note, *Romania* vol. xxxii).
    Orguil feit hum*me*. Auanter sei des biens kil nad mie en sei.
                  Feind*re* sei altre kil est.
                  Cuntrouer nuueleries.
                  Estriuer sanz encheisun etc.
    Ends f. 120 *b*: Dissolut et desafeite.
    The seventeenth is an extract from Jerome ad Demetriadem f. 163.
    The nineteenth a gloss on parts of the Sentences.
    There are some twenty of these tracts.
6. De septem sacramentis 181
    Sciendum quod septem sunt sacramenta ecclesie.
    Ends with questions on the Eucharist f. 215 *b*
    Quod si non possit non celebret.

I. 4. 5   C. M. A. 124

84. MEMORIAE SANCTORUM.

Vellum, 6⅛ × 4½, ff. 45, 20 lines to a page. Cent. xv late, written
in France for Scotch use.

Ex dono Josuae Barnes S.T.P. G(raecae) L(inguae) P(rofessoris) R(egii).

Collation: 1¹² (wants 1–3, 5: 11, 12) 2⁴ 3⁸ (wants 1) 4⁸ 5¹⁰
(2 canc.) 6¹⁰ (wants 8, 10) | 7⁷ (three left).

Contents :

1. Kalendar in red, blue and gold, wanting Jan., Feb., Mar.,
    May, Nov., Dec. . . . . . : . . . f. 1
    Each page has a partial border in which has been a small
    picture: all these have been excised.
    Ap. 9. Hugonis Archiep.
        30. Eutropii M.
    Mar. 16. Constantini et peregrini.
        21. Transl. eduardi regis.

July 15. Suytun Ep.
Aug.   5. Osuualdi R. M.
       30. Fiacri C.
       31. Transl. S. niniani Ep.
Sept. 4. Transl. S. Cuthberti.
       16. Niniani Ep. C. in gold.
2. In another hand (English?):
       Missus est Gabriel, a salutation to the Virgin . . f. 7
3. In the former foreign hand:
       A collection of Memoriae or suffrages to Saints viz.
       John Baptist   11
    Apostles. (Peter, Paul, Andrew, John, James mi., James ma.,
       Barthol., Matt., Simon, Jude.)
       De omnibus apostolis in verse.
       O petre beatissime apostolorum maxime .   .   .   (17) *b*
    Martyrs. Stephen, Laurence, Sebastian, George, Denis, Chris-
       topher, Erasmus. The Fifteen Helpers (George, Blaise,
       Erasmus, Pantaleon, Vitus, Christopher, Denis, Cyriac,
       Achatius, Eustace, Giles, Magnus, Margaret, Katherine,
       Barbara). All Martyrs.
    Confessors. Gregory, Jerome, Augustine, Ambrose, Martin,
       Nicholas, Antony, Benedict.
       Blaise. *Kentigern* (O Kentigerne gemma nobilis).
       Valentine. *Columba* (Salue sol Albanie).
       Duthacus Ep. (O Duthace pastor pie).
       Ninian (Stirps Regalis que vita floruit).
       All Confessors. The Three Kings.
    Virgins. Barbara, Margaret, Magdalene, Anne, Katherine.
       All Virgins.
    All Saints.
4. Three leaves (in a rather different hand) with rhyming poems
       to the Virgin.
    (*a*) Fragmentary.   ...(ue)hiculum.
                 tu limes equitatis, tu lumen claritatis
                 tu pauperis umbraculum
                 tu miseris latibulum
                 tu sceleris piaculum
                 tu limen ueritatis, tu lima prauitatis etc.
       Ends: Aue graciosa graciam implora
                 prece preciosa filium exora
                 adesto mortis hora. Amen.
    Resembles a poem by Joh. Francus in Milchsäck, *Hymni et
       Sequentiae*, 1886, no. 221.
    (*b*) Angelus ad uirginem, subintrans in conclaue.
    Printed with the original melody in *Arundel Hymns* ed. Duke
       of Norfolk and C. T. Gatty.
    (*c*) (M)ortis ut mors dilectio / qua dierum fit suaue / ut refert
       sancta lectio / nil est amanti graue.

I. 4. 6   C. M. A. 47

85. TRACT ON ROMISH CEREMONIES.

Vellum, 7 × 5, ff. 29, 18 lines to a page. Cent. xv, clearly written.
The cover consists of part of a leaf of a handsomely written
Canon Law MS. of cent. xiii.

Collation: a⁸ (wants 1, 8) b⁸–d⁸ (wants 8).

Inside the cover is :

> Wiclevi caeremoniarum Chronicon cujus initium deest.
> Balaeus de script. Brit. Cent. 6. 1.
>   G. Dill.

At the end :

> Christof*er* Watson Dunelmensis.
> Willm Andrewe(s?) of London m*ercer* A° 1539.

Then in Watson's hand (?)

> I judg thes collections (for diuers causes) to be Jhon Wycliffes
> ..c/th/es..

In Bale's notebook, ed. Poole and Bateson, p. 267, under Wycliffe
is this note

> Collegit ceremoniarum chronicon li. 1.   Alexander papa ordinauit primum.

Bale takes this "Ex domo Gul. Fluyd Cantabrigie." The
editor's note is "lost according to Shirley p. 50: probably spurious."
The same title and incipit is in Tanner, p. 770 col. 2, near the
bottom.

The tract is on the ceremonies ordained by divers popes, their rela-
tions with England, and their transgressions. It begins imperfectly:

> Pope Sixtus (viz. 2^dus) ordeyned that masse schuld be sungyn on
> awters which was not doon bifore.
> After f. 7 a leaf is gone.   On ff. 9, 10 is the story of Pope Joan.
> Ends with a note of the Statute of Provisors 1304.
> God for his mercy bryng his peple to his ordinaunce.   Amen.
> Explicit hic finis libri.
> There are many marginal notes by Watson (?).

I. 4. 7   C. M. A. 48

86. SERMONES ETC.

Vellum, 6½ × 4½, ff. 204, 24 and 32 lines to a page. Cent. xii–
xiii, in several very good small hands.

From Holmcultram.

On f. 1 in large black letters:

> Liber S. Marie de holmcoltra*m*.

Also later:

> liber clxvii^{us} primus.
> Sermones diuersorum.   Item glosa super genesim.

Also the name:

> Rowland Chambers (xvi).

Collation: 1⁴ 2⁸ 3⁸ (one canc.) 4⁸ 5¹² 6⁶ (+ 1) 7⁸–14⁸ 15¹⁰–17¹⁰ 18¹²
19¹² 20¹⁴ 21⁸ 22⁶ 23⁶ (gap) 24⁶.

Contents:

1. ff. 1–4 have notes for Sermons.
    Aromata mentis affectus compassionis etc. . . . f.   1 *b*
    Pisces mundi in mari in flumine in stagno . . .   2 *b*
    etc.
2. Inc. glosa super genesim   5
    Cum aliquis passus angustias ardenter querit deum dicit ei
    deus Fiat lux.
    Ends ?unfinished f. 18 *b*:—inter turbulencias uiciorum me
    firmau*it.*
    On f. 5 is Sermones diuersorum.   Liber clxvii^{us} primus.
    Liber S. Marie de Holmo.
3. The rest of the volume contains so far as I can see nothing but
    Sermons in fasciculi by various hands.
    The first is: Iherusalem que edificatur ut ciuitas.   Ciuitas hec
    in quadro posita est   19
    Before f. 199 is a gap, and the last quire 199-204 has a series
    of connected sermons on Domus fuliginis, Domus decoris,
    Domus pacis and Domine dilexi decorem domus tue.
    Ends f. 204 *a*: ad cenam regis iusticie caritatis ueste indutos
    facit transire.

I. 4. 8

87. Biblia.

Vellum, 6¼ × 4⅜, ff. 387 + 1, double columns of 52 lines.
Cent. xiii, in a beautiful minute hand.   Initials mostly in blue with
red ornament.

Given by   ?

Collation: 1 flyleaf.   1¹⁶ (wants 1) 2¹⁶–10¹⁶ 11¹² 12⁸ | 13¹⁶–27¹⁶.

Contents :

Jerome's Prologues. *a.* Frater Ambrosius, wanting the first leaf . f.   2
               b. Desiderii mei   3
Genesis (red and blue initial) to 2 Chron. (without Prayer of Manasses)   3 *b*
Esdr., Neem., etc.—Job.
Psalter with prologue, Psalterium Rome dudum positus.
    f. 163 *b* blank.
Prov.—Ecclus. Oratio Salomonis.
Isa.—Malachi. 1, 2 Macc.
Evv., Act., Paul. Epp., Cath. Epp., Apoc.
Interpretationes nominum. Aaz apprehendens   384
In triple columns, ends imperfectly in letter E.

I. 4. 9
88.

Paper, 7⅜ × 4⅝, ff. 10.   Cent. xvii, neatly written.
Perhaps from Sancroft.

Epitome Fidei et Religionis Turcicae...Autore Alb. Boborio.
Muhamed cum 40ᵐ aetatis suae annum attigisset
—ad coelestem gloriam insequentur.

I. 4. 10
89.

Paper, 6½ × 4¼, ff. 21.   Cent. xvi, xvii, neatly written.
Dedicated to John Overall, D.D., Regius Professor of Divinity,
by Ar. Harbert.

Copy of Letter of the King of Scotland sent into England
anno 1584, with the occasion thereoff brefle premised.
It is a credential of Harbert.
Scotica Nobilitas.   A tract in Latin beginning with

      Carolus Jacobus Stewartus Scotorum eius nominis rex sextus

ending with

      Carlilius dominus.

Lines by James VI on his mother's death, with English version.

I. 4. 11

90.

Paper, $6\frac{1}{8} \times 4\frac{3}{4}$, ff. 52.   Cent. xvi, very well written.
Vellum cover with gold tooling.
Given in 1691 by Lucas Milbourne ad Garienis ostium (Yarmouth) in Agro Norfolciensi Presbyter.
Dedication in Latin to Sir Walter Mildmay by Richard Clerk.
Acrostich on the motto *Virtute non vi*, and epigrams in Greek, Hebrew and Syriac.

The Gospel of St Mark in Greek and Hebrew, in parallel columns.

The Dedication says that the book was presented 7 Kal. Maii (near St Mark's Day) but does not mention the year : a previous gift of a metrical version of the Psalms in Greek is mentioned.

I. 4. 12   C. M. A. 78

91. RABANUS IN MATTHAEUM.

Vellum, $6\frac{1}{4} \times 4\frac{1}{8}$, ff. 203 + 3, 32 lines to a page.   Cent. xii, xiii,
clearly written.   2 fo. abeuntes humanitati.
Ex dono Rodolphi Cudworth 1600.
From Norwich (?).   At top of f. 1 : v. xlix.

Rodolphus Cudworth Collegio Emmanuelis dedit anno 1600.

Collation : 1 flyleaf.   a² 1⁸–25⁸ 26² (+ 1).

Contents :

1. Inc. capitula secundum Matheum . . . . f. i
    Liber generationis Ihesu Christi.   i.
    Vndecim discipuli abierunt.   lxxx.
    Expl. capit. libri mathei euangeliste.
    Rabanus super Matheum 1
    Prol.   Dominus ac redemptor noster ad commendationem
          —tum per regnum tum per eius diuinitatem.
    Matheus ex iudea sicut in ordine primus preponitur . . 3 *b*
    Ends f. 202 : Cuius hereditatis participes nos faciat d. n.
      I. C. cui honor laus et gloria per infinita seculorum secula.
      Amen.

Expl. euangelium Mathei cum expositione eiusdem.

2. Inc. prologus ysidori super euangelium Mathei . . . f. 202
Quatuor euangeliste dominum I. C. sub quatuor animalium uultibus
—concendere ut aquila.

3. Versus de euangelistis 202

Hic matheus agens hominem generaliter implet
Marcus ut alta fremit uox per deserta leonis
Jura sacerdocii lucas tenet ore iuuenci
More uolans aquile uerbo petit astra iohannes.

Matheus habet duo milia et septingentos uersus.
(Mc. 1700 Lc. 3800 Jo. (blank).)
Matheus intelligitur in homine quia circa humanitatem Christi
etc.
Cleros grece sors latine uel hereditas domini dicitur . . 202 b
Other notes, on antistes etc.
Inc. genealogia de ortu et obitu patrum 203
Adam pater generis humani manu dei ex terra formatus
etc.
—Melchisedech ... positus est in sua ciuitate que
sunt (fuit) salem postea.
Quot sunt sacramenta ecclesie etc.
Ad leuandum puerum de fonte tres ad plus recipiantur etc. 203
Verses on the ten commandments (4).

Dilige uicinum numen cole sabbata serua
Ne sis periurus dingne uenerare parentes
Ne sis occisor mecus fur testis inicus
Nec concupiscas. sic que sit lex tua disscas.

I. 4. 13   ? C. M. A. 34
92. HORAE.

Vellum, 6 × 4¼, ff. 199, 17 lines to a page. Cent. xv, early
English, in a beautiful narrow tall hand, with admirable ornaments.
Collation: 1⁶ 2⁸–6⁸ 7⁶ 8⁸–15⁸ (wants 7) 16⁸–25⁸ 26⁴ (wants 4).

Contents :

The Kalendar points to London. It has Ap. 30, Erkenwald in red. May 9, Transl. of S. Nicholas in red. Oct. 11, Ethelburga V. Nov. 14, Erkenwold. David, Chad and Wenefreda also occur.

There are notes of cent. xvi, as follows :

Jan. Thys daye William Newbolde son of Thomas Newbold was borne in Chaster-fel(d) beinge the xxiith daye of this month.

Mar. Ego Simon Newbold natus eram ad horam undecimam, viz. xxiiii die mensis Marcii post merid. illius diei a. d. mill. quingentesimo vicesimo qua(rto) die Jovis.

May. My father Will. Newbolde dyed betw,ene i & ii of the clocke in the afternone of the Satterday beinge the viith daye of Maye in the yere of owre lord MV^cXLI ... xxx ... Hen. 8 ... on whose sowle God haue mercy the signe then (?) beinge in Scorpio beinge of the age of lxiii & more (?).

June. Death of my suster Blythe then beinge at Caleys. 15 June 1544. aged 16... and lieth beried in colchurche.

Aug. Ego leofricus fforster natus eram iiii^o die Aug. 1520 die Jouis etc. The Litany closely resembles that in I. 2. 20. *Martyrs:* Edward, Alanus, Lambért, Julian. *Confessors:* Swithun, Remigius, Vedastus, Bavo, Audoen, Dunstan, ' Columbe,' Philibert, Botulph, Amandus. *Virgins:* Genovefa, Sexburga, Milburga, Ossatha.

The ornament, which consists entirely of borders and initials, is most admirable of its kind, and thoroughly English. I have seen very few better examples of the particular style than the decoration of the first page of the Hours (f. 7).

I. 4. 14
93.

Paper, 6 × 4¼, pp. 382.   Cent. xvii, neatly written.
On the flyleaves :

Ad usum fratris Laurentii Brien et conuentus de Cauan.

A poem :

> Ramillete de nuestra sennora.
>
> En un portal en Belem
> a la inclemencia del yelo
> estaua la virgen pura
> un ramilete texiendo.

Contents :

I. 4. 15   C. M. A. 77

94. T. A KEMPIS.

Vellum, $5\frac{9}{16} \times 3\frac{5}{9}$, ff. 108, 25 lines to a page. Cent. xv late, in a pretty hand, probably Flemish.

On f. 2 b, Gregorius Man.

On the last leaf:

Thomas Godsalue hunc librum dono dedit Ricardo Redmayne xvij° die mensis Aprilis 1531.

Reuerendissimus pater in Christo Will. Huddylstone Stratfordie abbas hunc librum dono dedit ffratri Joanni Meryoto 1533 (or 1523).

Collation: $1^2 \ 2^8$–$14^8 \ 15^4$ (wants 3, 4).

Contents :

Books III and IV of the De Imitatione Christi :
(Lib. III.) 1. Capitula subsequencia huius libelli (64) . . f. 1
   Handsomely bordered page.
   De interna Christi locucione ad animam fidelem . 3
   Audiam quod loquatur in me dominus Deus.
   O Beata anima que dominum in se loquentem audit.
   Ends f. 74 b: dirige per uiam pacis ad patriam
   perpetue claritatis. Amen. Expl.
(Lib. IV.) 2. Capitula de uenerabili sacramento (18) . . 75
   Ammoniciones de sacramento cum quanta re-
   uerencia Christus sit suscipiendus . . . 76
   Uenite ad me omnes qui laboratis
   —non essent mirabilia nec ineffabilia
   dicenda. Expl. hoc opusculum.

I. 4. 16

95. MEDICA.

Paper, 6 × 4¼, ff. 60 + 10, 21 lines to a page. Cent. xv, roughly written.

On the flyleaf is a draft of a letter.

Enquire of John ffurbancke of South hastead for one Henry Merinton and bring mee the townes name where hee dwelleth and whether he keepeth house & cattell and in what fashion he liueth. Likewise for Nicholas Place of Colchester and tell him I would entreat him to send mee some money by the bearer hereof Roberte Hancocke and tell him I had thought he would haue beene honest. I am still in prison and he know the missery of a prisoner and rest.   Yo^r very loving freind   Thomas Springe.

Contents :

Part of a book of Receipts in English.
The oldest foliation runs from 30—42, 48—90, 43, 44 (?).
The hand varies a good deal: the collection appears quite mis-
cellaneous.
At the end are some leaves of cent. xvii, with a table of contents,
receipts, and various scribbles and names. Maldon, Grantham,
Stamford are mentioned.

I. 4. 17

Paper, 6 × 3½, pp. 178 written, many blank. Cent. xvii.
On flyleaf :

Homo cum sis id fac semper intellegas. Tho. Holbeach.

Miscellaneous notes.

A declaracion of Dr White Bp. of Carlile touching the approba-
cion of Mr Richard Mountague his Appeale, presented to y^e
Right Rev^d ffather in God, the Lord Bp of Winchester .   .   f. 1

At the other end a leaf of notes from the Acts of the Apostles.

I. 4. 18

96.

Paper, $5\frac{3}{4} \times 3\frac{3}{4}$, pp. 176 and 37.   Cent. xvii.   Perhaps from
Sancroft.

Contents:

I. 4. 19

97.

Paper, $5\frac{3}{4} \times 3\frac{1}{2}$, ff. circ. 100 written, the rest blank.   Cent. xvii,
Sancroft's hand on the flyleaf.

A Catalogue of all the Prouosts, Fellows and Schollers of the Kings Colledge of the
blessed Virgin Mary and St Nicholas in the University of Cambridge [collected by
Thomas Hatcher to y^e year...and continued by N. W. [*this added by Sancroft*].

The original hand seems to go down to 1620, the continuation to 1640. There are notes in several hands. Several copies of this are in MS. at King's College and elsewhere. It was used by Harwood as the basis of his *Alumni Etonenses*.

I. 4. 20   C. M. A. 128

98.

Paper, 6¼ × 4, ff. 90–100, very neatly written. 1606. Vellum wrapper. Bequeathed by John Breton, D.D., Master.

Decla(ra)tion de la vraye obseruance et intention spirituelle de la Reigle de notre Pere S. Francois; faicte par vn de ses douze premiers compagnons appellé Frere Ange Tangredi prie des Freres de ce temps la. Traduicte d'Italien en Francois le 15 d'Auril 1606.
Au deuot Lecteur
 Il faut scauoir (ô deuot Lecteur).
Prologue. Combien que par plusieurs fois mayes prie.
Text. Pour la plus grande utilité des hommes il pleut a la diuine Maiesté.
In twelve chapters ending: il puissent viure et regner auec J. C. par tous les siecles des siecles. Amen.

I. 4. 21

99. STATUTES.

Vellum, 5¾ × 4, ff. 111, 31 lines to a page. Cent. xiv early, very neatly written. Two volumes, the second printed. Given by Th. Leigh. On f. 1

Henricus Gocheus.

At the end

Iste liber constat Thome Elton (xv). Iste liber constat Joh. Tindall (xv, xvi).

Collation: a² 1⁸ 2¹⁰ 3⁴ 4¹⁰ (10 canc.) 5¹⁰–9¹⁰ 10⁸ 11⁸ 12¹² (wants 10, 11) 13⁴.

Contents :

Magna Carta.
Carta de fforesta.
Sentencia lata super cartas.
Provisiones de Merton.
Stat. de Marlebergh . . . . f. 19
Stat. Westm. i (French).
Stat. de Mercatoribus (French) 32
Stat. Westm. ii.
Explanaciones articulorum . . . . 56 b
Stat. Wynton (French) 57
Stat. de Religiosis.
Stat. de Finibus.
Stat. de coniunctim feoffœtis 62
Stat. Westm. iii.
Articuli super cartas (French).
Stat. Lincoln. de Escaetoribus.
„   „   de Vicecomitibus (French).
Statutum Ebor. anno R. Ed. secundi septimo . . . . 71 b
De forinsecis vocatis ad warantum in hustengo London.
De apportis Religiosorum.
De vocatis ad warantum.
Nouum de foresta.
De Hibernia.
De frangentibus prisonam.
De conspiratoribus.
De assisa panis et ceruisie.
De exposicione vocabulorum.
De prerogatiua regis.
De Wardis et releuiis.
De quo waranto nouo.
De regia prohibicione.
Circumspecte agatis.
Iuramentum vicecomitum.
Ordo faciendi homagium etc.
Coment vileyn fra feaute a sen seignur.
Composicio monete.
Extenta manerii.
De Moneta.
Articuli eiusdem stat.
De Bigamis.
De Scaccario begins imperfectly 90
Districciones eiusdem.
Dies communes in Banco.
Dies dotis.
Composicio facta ad puniend. infringentes assisam forestallar'.
De ulnis et bussellis.
De fforstallariis.
De quo waranto iii.

Ragman.
In quibus casibus in antiq. dominicis corone capienda est assisa
noue dis.
De terris templariorum (17 Ed. II).
Visus franci plegii,
De essonio calumpniando.
De appellatis.
De Iustic. assign.
De frangentibus prisonam.
Composicio ulnarum et perticarum.
De malefactoribus in parcis.
De proteccionibus.
Modus leuandi fines.
De gauelet'. de militibus.
Stat. Exon.
Come hugh le despenser.
Notes and verses at the end.
Vol. ii is a printed book.   The Rates of the Custome house etc.
London, John Allde, 1582.

I. 4. 22

100.

Paper, 6⅞ × 4¼, ff. 13.   Cent. xvii.
Binding: fragment of a leaf of service-book of cent. xv, with
music.

A short cathechisme which conteineth a declaration of the true waie to life everlastinge
meet of everie one to be knowen before they be admitted to the supper of the lorde.   8 ff.
List of Bible texts.
Some private accounts.

I. 4. 23

101.

Paper, 5¾ × 3¾, ff. circ. 200.   Cent. xvi.

A collection of Coats of Arms (English) neatly drawn.   A good many are blank,
and a good many unnamed.
The first are the Arms of University College, Oxford, Edward the Confessor, Merton
College, Sir Thomas Pope.
The last Monsʳ John Deverose.

I. 4. 25

102. BIBLIA.

Vellum, 4¾ × 3⅝, ff. 483, double columns of 54 lines.   Cent. xiii, in a good minute hand.

Binding: white vellum of cent. xvi, with gold tooling, and the words DONVM CANDIDVM in gold on each side. This I conjecture is a pun on the name of Whitgift. Probably the Archbishop made a present of the book to a friend.

Ex dono Rev^{di} Gul. Gibbon, A.M. 1731.

Collation: 1^{22} 2^{24}–5^{24} 6^{26} 7^{24} (+ 1) 8^{24} 9^{20} 10^4 | 11^{20}–15^{20} 16^{26} 17^{24}– 21^{24} 22^{18} 23^2.

Contents:

Prologues of Jerome.
Genesis—2 Chron. Prayer of Manasses follows without break.
Ezra, Nehemiah, 1 Esdras (=3 Esdras), Tob., Judith, Esther, Job.
Quicunque vult and notes from Augustine.
Gallican Psalter, and Hymns for Nocturnes.
Prov.—Ecclus., Isa.—Malachi, 1, 2 Macc.
Gospels, Paul. Epp., Acts, Cath. Epp., Apoc.
Interpretationes nominum. Aaz—Zuzim.
Table of Gospels for the year, unfinished: in another hand.

Figured initials:

1. *Prologue.* Jerome writing.
2. *Genesis.* Seven quatrefoils in medallion. *a.* Creation of light. *b.* Separation of land and water. (In these Christ holds globe.) *c.* Christ between trees. *d.* Holding Sun and Moon. *e.* Birds and beasts on R. *f.* Creation of Eve. *g.* Christ resting. At bottom. Crucifixion with the Virgin and St John.
3. *Psalter.* David plays harp.
The rest are decorative.

I. 4. 26   C. M. A. 97

103. STATUTA EDWARDI III.

Vellum, 4¾ × 3¾, ff. 209, 20 lines to a page.   Cent. xiv early, neatly written.

Given by Tho. Leigh.

Collation: 1^8 (wants 8) 2^8–7^8 8^8 (+6 after 7 : wants 8) 9^8–23^8 24^{12} 25^{10}.

Contents :

> Statuta Edwardi III. Anno I–XLV.
> Come hugh le Despenser . . . . f. I
> The hand changes at f. 188.
> The last Statute begins :
> (E)n parlement semous a Wincestr'.

The whole text is in French.

I. 4. 27

104.

Paper, $4\frac{7}{8} \times 2\frac{3}{4}$, ff. 56 written.   Cent. xvii.   From Sancroft.

The Relation of the desperate state of Francis Spira collected by Sr Francis Bacon. With Preface by Bacon.

At the end : Anno domini 1637.

I. 4. 28

105.

Paper, $4\frac{5}{8} \times 2\frac{3}{4}$, ff. circ. 70 written, side ways (parallel with the height of the book).   Cent. xvii, late.   From Sancroft or Barnes.

A collection of Latin Epigrams, 447 in number.

The principal sources are, Owen's Epigrams, 1–220; Zevecotius, 222–247; Banhusius, 242–315. Anon. and Miscellaneous. The last is from Philpot's Remains.

I. 4. 31

106. DEVOTIONS, ETC.

Vellum, $4\frac{3}{8} \times 3$, ff. 196, 23 lines to a page.   Cent. xiv, in a pretty hand, with good ornaments.   Written in England (Worcestershire ?).

Collation : 1^{87} (wants 1–3) 2^8–9^8 (wants 1) 10^8–25^8.

Contents :

> 1. Selections from a treatise (? the Elucidarius) in French . f. I
> Beginning imperfectly : the first rubric (f. 1) is
> Coment se tienent le solail et la lune et les estoilles en ciel.
> Cap. ccx^{mo}.

Les planetes sunt du firmament et tut en semble se tienent.
Then follow chapters 211 (hours of day and night), 212 (move-
ment of stars), 246 (the complexions), 285 (complexions of
planets and signs), 338 (where Noah's ark rested), 29 (man
made in God's image), 34-37, 66, 67, 77, 88: then two un-
numbered sections, the second: le quel profite plus al alme
ceo que home doune de lalmoigne en ceste secle ou ceo que
home fra pur lui.

2. Poem (written as prose, as is nearly all the verse in this book)   f. 10

      Greuous mal est de peccher
      Et pier est de pecche trop amer,
      Mes uncore est plus greuous
      Quant le pecche turne en us.
Ends: Et nos pecches lesser nectement.
      Amen Amen sige we
      Olde and ȝounge par charite Amen.
3. Poem.   Mon queor me dist que doi amer .   .   .   11 b
      Mes ieo ne sai ou empler.
Ends: Douz ihesu fontaine de uie
      Qui garist de langour
      En qui soule ioie est acomplie
      La fycherai mamur. Amen.

4. Ces sunt les uendredis que sunt tous a iuner .   .   .   12
   Jeo clement romain euesque a toutz les fedaus dieu salutz
      —Abraham sacrifia soen fiz ysaac.
   This paragraph on the twelve Fridays exists in Greek and
   Latin: printed by Mercati in *Notizie et testi d. Lett. Crist.
   antica.* Greek at Trinity College (MS. O. 8. 33).
5. Poem. A Ihesu ameez si amerai vous e dedenz a mon queor
      donetz leesce .   .   .   .   12 b
      Tut seit il que moun corps dehors soefre hunte et tristesce.
   Ends. Et puisse uous od tut le cors tut dis emsemblement.
6. Ci commence le office des Mors .   .   .   .   .   .   13 b
7. Oratio S. Thome de Aquino.   Concede michi queso misericors
      deus   26
8. Prayers. *a.* for a traveller (including Deus qui beatos tres magos)   27
      b. Si uous estes en pecche mortele: (the Five Wounds) .   27 b
9. Ci commence le beau dit de nostre dame que est apelle le
      renome de renty .   .   .   .   28 b

      Reigne de pite marie
      en que la deite pure et chere
      a mortalite se marie
      tu es uierge fille et mere.

   Ends: de lui gaynet gre et grace. Amen.
10. Prayers. *a.* Nous troums en escrit / que le mort a uif dit / il
    nad en munde si grant peccheur / ne si maueis lechur / qui

trei fez le iour / dirra ceste oreisun / que deu de lui a chef de
iur / nauera pardun . . . . f. 30
    Dame seinte marie uirgine et genitere: ends in Latin.
  b. Beau sire deu omnipotent / merci vous cri mult humblement   30 *b*
  c. Les cinc ioies N.D. Aue seinte mere corone . . 34 *b*
  d. (Address of Christ on the Cross.) Tu qui esgardes ma
    figure / Jeo su deu tu ma facture 36
  e. Sabbato celebretur de B.V. et quare 37
  In septima feria de B.V. inicium habuit
    —deus ab omni opere requieuit.

11. Devotional tract, dialogue of soul and man 38
  Exurge quare obdormis anima mea exurge
    —nomen domini inuocabo.

12. Letania. *Martyrs.* Edmund, Kenelm, Thomas. *Confessors.*
  Dunstan, Edmund 42
  Virgins. Brigida.
  Prayers. Domine—qui ad principium huius diei . . . 45 *b*
    Sancta Maria mater domini .
    Dirigere et sanctificare.

13. Poem. Ki ceste escrit uoil entendre / Grand ben il purra apprendre   46
  Ends: Deu nous donne sa grace / Que fere puissons en
  chescune place / Sa uolunte et soen pleiser / Dreit ben fer a
  chescun ber. Amen.

14. The good wife . . . . 48 *b*
  þe gode wif tauhte hire douster fele sithe and ofte.
  Douster ӡif þou wilt ben a wif and wisliche to wirche.
  Ends. Here blessinge mote þou haue and wel mote þou þriue.
  Wel is þe child þat þriue mai. Mi leue child.

15. Story of a pope whose mother killed her child; her appearance
  after death, and liberation from purgatory . . . 52
  Un apostoille iadis estoit
    —servunt sauuez des touz perils. Amen. ff. 54, 55 blank.

16. Kalendar in black, pink and red 56
  Jan. 19. Wlstan in red.
  Mar. 1, 2. David and Chad original. 18, 20. Edward KM.
  Cuthbert, in red.
  Ap. 2. Richard in red.
  May. Dunstan, Aldelm, Augustine in red.
  June 7. Transl. S. Wlstani Ep. in red.
  Oct. 2. S. Thome Herford in red. 6. Transl. S. Hugonis
  in red. 13. Transl. S. (erasure) in red. 15. Wlfranni
  Ep. in red.
  The importance attached to Wulstan and his translation
  points to Worcester.
  A leaf is gone after f. 61. On f. 62 is a partial border of very
  good work, and an initial with a figure of St Paul seated
  with sword.

17. Tract. Des treis degres de contemplacion 62

Videte uocationem uestram. Ceste mot de lapostle partient a nous genz de religion.
On f. 97 *b*, 98 : pur ceo dist un engleis en tiele manere de pite.
Nou goth þe sonne under wode. Me riweth marie þi faire rode.
Nou goth sonne under tre. Me riweth marie þi sone and þe.
Ends f. 105 *b* : Et ceste sacrament ausi offre seint eglise pur les leaus morts qui mestier unt de aide a ceo que ele croit.

18. Ces sunt les proverbes de sages philosophes. Partial border very good . . . . f. 106
Dauid dist en soen liure / Que commencement de bien uiure.
Seneca, Sidrac, Salomon, Ieremias, Ruben, Nabugodonosor, Abimelec, Libanus, etc. are quoted. Ends f. 114 : que ceus que lirrunt ceste escrit / En breues paroles eyent delit.

19. Poem. Ki prodhome estre uoldra / Sanz trauail pas ne serra　124
Moral precept : ends f. 118 *b* : que le home het lautre a graunt tort / Come si il eust soen parent mort.

20. Tract : dialogue between a Father and Son : excellent border and initial 119
Beau fiz mult ad deu feel pur totes genz par sa grand curtesie.
Ends with exposition of Gloria in excelsis : f. 142 : pais en terre et la glorie en ciel. quod nobis prestare dignetur qui uiuit in sec. sec. There is a change of hand at f. 141.

21. Story of the monk who listened to a bird's (angel's) song for 300 years 142
Ore nous dirroms un bone ensample
—nous serroms parciner de la ioie.

22. Ici commence une profitable treite de confession. Border and initial. In verse . . . . 144 *b*
Dusze choses couendra auer / qui dreit se uoudra confesser.
Seems to end at f. 174 *b* : mult deuoms dunques amer / oreisun q*ue* est de si grant poer.
Contains many stories.

23. Possibly a continuation, but with a large initial . . . 174 *b*
Tucher couient en tute guise / Chose que tuche seinte eglise.
Story of Belshazzar etc. : ends f. 179 *b* : user en seculier seruise / ffere nel deuetz en nulle guise.

24. To the Virgin. Beneite seit tu marie / mere de pite . . 179 *b*
—et nous ameine a sun pais / apres le horrible iugement.
Note in Latin of indulgences by John XXII etc. . . 180

25. Ici commencent les lamentations nostre dame, in prose . 181
A Deu qui me durra taunt des lermes.
—vous seiet beneite od uostre fiz qui est et serra ouesques li pere et li seint espirit un deux per omnia sec. sec. Amen.
Oratio ad patrem. Deus in cuius ditione cuncta sunt . . 190
Or. bona ad d. I. C. Saluator mundi saluum me fac . . 190 *b*
Alia or. ad angelum gubernatorem. Obsecro te angelice spiritus　191
Memoriae of SS. John Baptist, Christopher, Anne, Mary Magd., Katherine, Margaret . . . . 191 *b*

26. In another hand.
Cy comence la passion nostre seignour translate de latin
en Romaunce   .   .   .   .   f. 193
Ceo auient el quinzime an que Tyberis Cesar aueit este Emperour.
The Gospel of Nicodemus, ending imperfectly f. 196 *b* (which
is very faint).

I. 4. 32   vac.

107. CONSTITUTIONES PROVINCIALES.

Vellum, 4⅝ × 3, ff. 113, 25 lines to a page. Cent. xv, very well
written, with headlines and marginalia in blue.

Given by Abp Sancroft : on f. 1 is W. Sancroft.

Collation : $1^8-7^8\ 8^{710}$ (wants 5, 6, 10) $9^8-13^8\ 14^{10}$.

Contents :

Constitutiones prouinciales.
De summa Trinitate et fide catholica   .   .   .   .   . f.   1
Firmiter credimus et simpliciter confitemur.
Quire 8 ff. 57–63 is out of place, for contents see below : f. 64
follows 56 immediately : there is a gap after f. 79.
Ends de decimis : Decime tributa sunt egentium animarum
—sed hominum malicia prohibet.
Quire 8 contains Termini apud Westmonasterium.
Periculum animarum peruicatorum.
Iuramentum procuratoris, aduocati, scribe.
Quoniam priuilegiati tenentur ostendere sua priuilegia (imperfect).

I. 4. 33   vac.

108. N.T. IN ENGLISH.

Vellum (uterine), 4 × 2¾, ff. 346 + 2, double columns of 31 lines.
Cent. xiv, xv, very finely written.

Given by Abp Sancroft. "G. S. Archiep. Cantuar. legavit
Collegio Emman. Cantabr."

On the flyleaves :

(*a*) Ex dono Thome Hughes de Lincolnes Inne armigeri fratris mei charissimi.
17 Sep.
(*b*) Thomas Ken (probably the Bishop of Bath and Wells).
(*c*) Erased.

Collation : 1² 2⁸ 3⁸ | 4¹² (wants 12) 5² (a supply of cent. xvi) 6¹²– 17¹² (9, 10 much later) 18¹² (one canc. in 2nd half) 19¹² 20¹² (7 torn) 21¹² 22¹² (8 torn) 23¹² (1 torn) 24¹² (2, 4 torn) 25¹²–29¹² (wants 1, 2 : 9 torn) 30¹² (wants 5 + 1) 31¹⁴ 32⁴ (supply of cent. xvi).

Contents :

I. 4. 34   vac.

109. GREEK SERVICE-BOOK.

Paper, 4 × 3, ff. 133 + 2, 20 lines to a page. Cent. xvii (1694) in several hands, some good.

In the earlier part every page has an ornamental border in red.

Given by Abp Sancroft. W. Sancroft is on f. 1.

On the flyleaves :

Extract from Josephus *Antiq.* I. 3. 3. περὶ τῶν τοῦ Σήθου στηλῶν. Σοφίαν τὴν περί— Συριάδα. This recurs later on in the book.

Contents:

I. 4. 35   C. M. A. 3

110. EPISTOLAE PAULI GRAECE.

Vellum, 3⅝ × 3⅛, ff. 144 + 1, 24 lines to a page. Cent. x, xi
(Gregory says xii), in a most beautiful minute hand, hanging from
lines ruled with a dry point.

On the flyleaf:

Collegio Emmanuelis in testimonium grati animi D.D. Samuel Wright eiusdem
Collegii Alumnus Anno 1598 Pridie nonas Iulias.

(The original inscription, now very faint, is copied below.)

Collation: 1 flyleaf.   1⁸ | gap | 2⁸-6⁸ | gap | 7⁸ 8⁸ (4, 5 misbound
after f. 2 of quire 9) 9⁸ 10⁸ (4, 5 bound after f. 131) 11⁸-18⁸.

Contents:

1.   The Catholic Epistles beginning probably in 2 Pet. ii. 1 (the
     upper half of the first page is almost totally illegible as far as
     verse 4) ending with 1 Jo. iii. 20. μείζων ἐστὶν ὁ θεὸς τῆς
     καρδίας.

2. The Pauline Epistles beginning in the Argument to the Epistle
to the Romans .   .   .   . f.   9
ἐλθεῖν διὰ τὸν εἰς αὐτοὺς πόθον.
The arguments and κεφάλαια are written throughout in beautiful
semi-uncials.
There is a gap after ἀνὴρ μὲν γὰρ οὐκ ὀφεί / (1 Cor. xi. 7)
to 1 Cor. xv. 56 θανάτου ἡ ἁμαρτία.
A second hand not quite so good as the first begins near the
bottom of f. 114 a (1 Tim. vi. 5) and continues to the end.
Ends imperfectly Heb. xi. 27 θυμὸν τοῦ βασιλέως τὸν γὰρ.
An interesting point is that on f. 109 b and in one or two other
places there are Latin glosses in old pencil which cannot be
much later than cent. xiii. The only one I can read clearly
is on f. 109 b *hedificacione* which is a note on the reading
μᾶλλον ἢ οἰκοδομίαν (for οἰκονομίαν) in 1 Tim. i. 4. Another
on 1 Tim. iii. 10 ἀνέγκλητοι ὄντες begins *nullum* (?) *crimen
habentes.* This must mean that the MS. has been in Western
Europe, if not in England, since mediaeval times. In the
list of Cursive MSS. (Gregory *Proll. in N.T.*) it ranks as
Act. 53, Paul. 30. Various readings from it were given in
Walton's *Polyglott.* In Mill's edition it ranked as Cant. 3.
It was collated by Scrivener in 1855, who calls it *n.* He
gives a facsimile of some lines in his *Introduction* (pl. XII.
no. 33). Dr Hort examined it, and Gregory saw it in 1883.

I. 4. 36
111.

Paper, 6 × 4, ff. circ. 160. Cent. xvii, rather well written.
In the cover the name Johan. Balderston.
At one end : some undergraduate's private accounts.

Notes on Homer's *Iliad.*
A longish tract in Latin: philosophical.
Actum est tum de definitione cum de divisione quantitatis.

At the other end :

Notes on words in the Greek text of the New Testament.

II. I. I   C. M. A. 68
112. GREGORII MORALIA.

Vellum, 19½ × 12, ff. 223, double columns of 70 lines. Cent. xiv,
in a fine hand, with most beautiful ornaments. English work of
the best type. Sadly mutilated by the excision of leaves and initials.

E. C. C.   7

Collation: a¹² (wants 2) b¹² (wants 3) c¹² d¹² (wants 7) e¹² f¹² g¹²
(wants 9) h¹² i¹² k¹² (wants 1, 2, 6–9) l¹² (wants 11, 12) m¹² (wants 9)
n¹² (wants 4, 5, 10) o¹² p¹² (wants 7, 12) q¹² (wants 6, 12) r¹² s¹² t¹²
(wants 7, 10) v⁸ (wants 1) x¹² (wants 2, 7): 21 quires.

At top of f. 1

Anno 1600 Collegio Emmanuelis Dedit Rodolph: Cudworth eiusdem Coll. Socius.

Contents:

Inc. prologus moralium beati Iob (the Visio Taionis).   .   . f.   1
    Beatus gregorius papa librum iob petente sancto Leandro
    ...quam uidit in ecclesia b. petri apostoli.
Hec uisio per totam hyspaniam scripta inuenitur principio moralium
    b. gregorii pape urbis rome.
Reuerentissimo atque sanctissimo fratri leandro coepiscopo gregorius
    seruus seruorum dei.
Dudum te pater beatissime in constantinopolitana urbe.
A leaf is lost, with the beginning of the commentary, after f. 1.
    There are many other lacunae, as the collation above shows,
    mostly at the beginnings of the books.
Ends (l. xxxv) f. 223 b: per eterna sec. sec. Amen.
Expliciunt b. gregorii moralia triginta quinque libris consummata.

The decoration of the volume is of the first class. The beginning
of each book has had a partial border and historiated initial; though
many of these have been cut out. The borders are solid bands of
pink and blue with cross-bands of gold: at intervals they spread
into broader fields of various shapes, and are always decorated with
oak-leaves, principally in pink and green. Birds and sometimes
figures are perched on the ends. The grounds of the pictured
initials are uniformly of gold with punctured patterns. The
draperies of the figures are in subdued colours, grey, pink, green,
blue, heightened copiously with white. The drawing admirable
throughout. Altogether a most notable example of English art.

It is not doubtful, from the presence of Benedictine monks in
initials and borders, that the book was written at or for a Benedictine
monastery. As others of Cudworth's MSS.[1] came from Norwich,
I conjecture that this is a Norwich book. It might be usefully
compared with the Ormesby Psalter in the Bodleian.

1. f. 1. Full border. On *R.* two birds, grey with black-ended wings, very
humorously drawn. *Initial to Prologue.* A king, attended by a clerk, faces an Archbishop and several Bishops on *R.* This is king "Chyndesuidus" at the Council of
Toledo admonishing the Bishops to get a copy of the *Moralia.*

[1] Viz. nos. 91, 142.

2. *Initial to dedication.* Gregory in tiara (tall mitre surrounded with crown) seated: Leander with mitre and crozier stands on *R.* Both wear chasubles.

On ff. 3, 3 *b*, 5 are decorative initials and partial borders.

3. Lib. II. f. 7. Christ with crossed nimbus and raised hands seated on *L.* On *R.* a crowd of kneeling figures, the foremost a monk in dark habit: the devil blue and bearded crouches on *R.* and pulls his robe. This represents the sons of God assembled and Satan among them.

f. 12 etc. decorative initials: leaf with beginning of Lib. III. gone after f. 13.

4. Lib. IV. Gregory seated on *L.* speaking. A black monk on *R.* holds open book.

5. Lib. V. Abraham (represented like Christ with cross-nimbus) seated on cloud. The soul of Lazarus nimbed stands in his lap. He has scroll: *Memento fili quia recepisti bona in uita tua, lazar(us)* (Luke xvi. 25). Below on *R.* hell-mouth. Dives in a caldron within it. The passage is quoted in the text.

6. Lib. VI. Border left, but initial cut out.

Lib. VII. First leaf gone.

7. Lib. VIII. A group of six knights in mail, beautifully drawn. They have pink and green surcoats, and bearings, probably imaginary, on their shields: e.g. one on *R.* has *azure* a chevron *arg.* surmounted by a cross, on chief parts of another chevron, on base a cross *arg.* suggesting another chevron. The text deals with the passage *Super pupillum irruitis* etc. (Job vi. 27).

8. Lib. IX. Devils falling into hell-mouth: a cloud above. Cf. Job iv. 18 in angelis suis reperit prauitatem.

Lib. X. Border left, initial cut out.

9. Lib. XI. Man in round cap on *L.* with scroll: *Nudus egressus sum de utero matris mee nudus reuertar illuc* (Job i. 21). Three men stand on *R.*

Lib. XII. First leaf gone.

10. Lib. XIII. Christ clad only in a garment about His middle bears the Cross (green and tau-shaped) to *R.* One man precedes, two follow. Cf. Job xvi. 11 percusserunt maxillam meam etc.

11. Lib. XIV. Job barefoot in white robe kneels on *R.* and looks back to *L.* where the devil with a birch rod is about to smite him. The devil is blue, hoofed, hook-nosed and bearded. Above in a cloud the Divine Hand. Job has a scroll: *Dominus dedit dominus abstulit sit nomen domini benedictum* (Job i. 21). Goldfinch in border.

12. Lib. XV. In border on *L.* a large figure of Gregory in tiara, chasuble, pall, dalmatic and alb, holding scroll, and pointing to *R.* On his scroll is: *Ducunt in bonis dies suos et in puncto ad inferna descendunt.* In the initial to which he points are two men seated conversing. The one on *L.* has a purse, the other wears gloves and appears to have a purse attached to his wrist. Below, the same two men plunge into hell-mouth.

13. Lib. XVI. Hezekiah, crowned, in bed. Over him stands Isaiah with scroll (rubbed): *Dispone domui tue (quia morieris et non) uiues* (Is. xxxviii. 1).

Lib. XVII., XVIII. First leaves gone.

14. Lib. XIX. Christ full-face throned on the rainbow, holding orb and blessing. He is in a quatrefoil with gold ground. In the spandrels on blue ground are the four Evangelistic emblems.

Lib. XX., XXI. First leaves gone.

15. Lib. XXII. Christ kneeling, girt with towel, washes Peter's *R.* foot, other Apostles on *R.* and *L.* Jay (?) in border.

The text deals with humility.

16. Lib. XXIII. The Virgin and Apostles kneeling on *L.* and Peter and Apostles kneeling on *R.* watch the ascending Christ, whose feet are seen in a cloud. Robin in border.

17. Lib. XXIV. The Nativity. The Virgin in bed (head to *L.*). Joseph seated on *R.* In front on *L.* the ass, the manger with the swaddled Child (cross-nimbed), the ox. Parrot in border, and peacock with fine gold tail.

18. Lib. XXV. Christ with book. Adam reclines on *L.*

19. Lib. XXVI. Christ with scroll : *Discite a me quia mitis sum et humilis corde* (Matt. xi. 29). In the border on *R.* two black monks kneeling, with joined hands, face *L.* Lib. XXVII., XXVIII. First leaf gone.

20. Lib. XXIX. On *L.* John preaching, with scroll: *In principio erat uerbum et uerbum erat apud deum et* (John i. 1). On *R.* a group of listeners seated on the ground. Above on cloud a half-length figure of Christ with book blessing.

21. Lib. XXX. Paul, beardless in pink robe, on his knees; sword lies by him. He has scroll : *Quis es domine* (Acts ix. 5). Above Christ half-length on cloud with scroll : *Saule, Saule, quid me persequeris* (Acts ix. 4).

22. Lib. XXXI. The Fall. Eve on *R.* eats and gives apple to Adam. The serpent human headed and with two legs is coiled about the tree above them, tail uppermost. Brown bird with black head in border.
Lib. XXXII.–XXXV. First leaves gone.

II. 1. 3   C. M. A. 6

113. GORHAM SUPER EPISTOLAS.

Vellum, $17\frac{1}{4} \times 12\frac{3}{8}$, ff. $335 + 3$, double columns of 60 lines. Cent. xv, well written and ornamented : in two hands.

2 fo. refundit.

Original binding: rough skin, once red, over bevelled wooden boards : two clasps gone : mark of chain staple below lower clasp on first cover.

Old list of contents inside cover.

Collation : 1 flyleaf. 1^8–7^8 8^6 9^8–18^8 19^4 20^8–38^8 39^{10} 40^8 41^8 42^{12} (1 canc.) 1 flyleaf.

Contents :

1. Nicholaus Gorram (Gorranus) super Epistolas Pauli.
      Prol. Dedi te in lucem gencium .   .   .   .   f.   1
   Good initial (blue, pink, orange and green, on gold) and border
      on three sides of characteristic English work.
   Ad Romanos. Initial and border as before   5
      1 Cor. f. 63. 2 Cor. f. 113. Gal. f. 147 (change of hand).
      Eph. f. 164 *b*. Phil. f. 182. Col. f. 196. 1 Thess. f. 209 *b*.
      2 Thess. f. 221 *b*. 1 Tim. f. 228 *b*. 2 Tim. f. 244 *b*. Tit.
      f. 255. Philem. f. 262. Heb. f. 264, ending f. 308 *b*:
      gloriam dabit dominus.

Expl. postille fratris N. super omnes epistolas Pauli. Deo gracias.
Each Epistle and Prologue thereto has a good initial and border.

2. Idem super Actus Apostolorum .   .   .   .   .   .   f. 309
    Scribe uisum et explana eum.
    Initial and border as usual. The hand is the first which
    occurred in the volume.
    Ends f. 355 *b*: martirio coronatus. Expl. actus apostolorum.
    A short notice of this MS. appeared in *Collectanea Topo-
    graphica* Vol. VIII., pp. *32 *34: a copy of the article
    (*Writings of N. Gorram*) is in the MS.

II. 1. 4   C. M. A. 45

114. PSALTERIUM GLOSATUM.

Vellum, 16¾ × 12¼, ff. 252, double columns (text and gloss inter-
mixed) of 57 lines at most. Cent. xii, very finely written.
Given by Tho. Leigh.   2 fo. -gentia clarescit.
Collation : 1⁸–32⁸ (wants 5–8).

Contents :

    Psalterium glosatum.
    Prol. Cum omnes prophetas .   .   .   .   .   .   f. 1
    —titulus talis.
    Inc. lib. ymnorum uel soliloquiorum prophete de Christo.
    Liber dicit et non libri.
    The text begins on f. 2.
    Beatus uir has a magnificent initial, principally in red and blue on
    gold ground, edged with green. The beginning of the gloss has
    also an excellent initial of smaller size.

The initials to the ordinary Psalms are in flat colours, usually
red and green and filled with ornament.

    Ps. xxvi. *Dominus illuminatio.* Half-figure nimbed and beardless on gold ground
with scroll : *Dns illuminatio* etc.—*quem timebo.*
    On the lower margin of f. 60 is part of a copy of a deed relating to Raunes (?)
Northamptonshire 27 Eliz.
    Dixi custodiam. Decorative with gold.
    Quid gloriaris. Decorative with gold.
    Dixit insipiens. Soldier in silver armour holding sword and head. Headless body
on *R.* standing.
    Saluum me fac. Decorative. Also *Exultate.*
    Cantate. David throned with sword inscribed *Rex Dauid*, kneeling figure on *R.*
with harp (?).

Domine exaudi. Tonsured man in green, white and red robe, with blue cloak or cope detached behind him, kneels facing *R*. Veiled altar with gold chalice. Gold ground. *Dixit Dominus.* A very beautiful decorative initial in flat colours without gold. At about f. 200 ornaments in black of skilful execution begin to appear in the lower margin attached to the text.
Ends imperfectly in Ps. cxlvii. qui emittit eloquium.
There are very many marginal notes in an excellent hand.

II. 1. 5

115. EPISTOLAE PAULI CUM GLOSSA (PETRI LOMBARDI).

Vellum, $17\frac{1}{2} \times 12\frac{1}{8}$, ff. 221, double columns of 59 lines (gloss).
Cent. xii, very well written and ornamented.   2 fo. data. quid.
Collation: 1^8–27^8 28^6 (wants 6).   The old foliation is incorrect.

Contents :

Pauli Epistolae glosatae.
Prol. Principia rerum requirenda sunt prius
   —salutationem dicens.
Fine initial with dragons etc. in red, blue, green and pink on a gold ground edged with green.
Each Epistle has an equally fine initial. The white lion-like animals which often occur in MSS. from Christ Church Canterbury are present in several: but the writing rather suggests St Albans.
Phil. f. 150 b: Paul on *L.* gives a blank scroll to a messenger.
Ends f. 222 (221) b: sit cum omnibus uobis amen.
A later scribble: Explicit hic liber uellem habere.

II. 1. 6   C. M. A. 43

116. BIBLIA.

Vellum, 16 × 10, ff. 349, double columns of 54 lines.   Cent. xiii (second half), in a very good hand, with fine historiated initials : has suffered serious mutilation.
Collation: 1 flyleaf, first quire gone. 2^{12}–6^{12} ‖ quire gone ‖ 7^{12}–14^{12} (wants 6, 7) 15^{12}–18^{12} ‖ quires gone ‖ 19^{12} ‖ quires gone ‖ 21^{12} 22^{12} (11 canc.) 23^{12}–28^{12} 29^{10} | 30^8 31^{10}.
The upper corner of the flyleaf has been cut off and replaced by a xvth cent. slip with some verses on the days of creation.

Prima dies celum format creat altera terram etc.

There are traces of erased inscriptions.

Contents :

Genesis, beginning imperfectly in xxxi. 25 in eodem monte Galaad.
Exodus—Joshua xxii. 32. 1 Reg. iv. 16—2 Paral. Prayer of
Manasses follows without a break.
Ezra, Nehemiah.
Inc. liber esdre secundus=4 Esdr. i. 11.
Liber esdre secundus=3 Esdr. (1 Esdr. of our Apocrypha).
Liber esdre quartus=4 Esdr. iii.-xiv. (in xi. chapters).
Liber esdre quintus=4 Esdr. xv., xvi.
Judith, Esther (ends in c. xiv.). Tobit (begins in vi. 7). Job.
Prologues to Psalter.   *a.* Dauid filius Iesse.
                         b. Psalterium Rome dudum.
                         c. Scio quosdam putare.
                         d. Psalterium quod secundum lxx.
Psalter in two parallel versions. Gallican on *L.* Roman on *R.*
Proverbs: ends in xii. 19.
Isaiah xxxvi. 9 to end.
Jeremiah i.-xii. 7.
Daniel iii. 2—Malachi.
1, 2 Macc.
Evv.
Acts: ending: quod hic est I. C. filius dei per quem incipiet totus
mundus iudicari.
Cath. Epp.
Paul. Epp.   Epistle to Laodiceans follows 2 Thess.
Apoc.: at end, Laus tibi sit Christe quia liber hic explicit iste.
Hic inc. interpretationes hebraicorum nominum secundum Remigium
incipientium per a litteram et primo post *a* sequitur *a* (sic).
In 4 columns to a page. Aaz—Zuzim.
Hic expl. interp. omnium nominorum hebreorum et syrorum seu
grecorum interpretatorum secundum Beatum Remigium incipien-
cium per singulas litteras alphabeti.
There are stichometric notes at the end of 1 Macc. Explicit liber
primus machabeorum habens uersus duo milia trescentos.
After 2 Macc.:
Expl. mach. lib. secundus uersus habens mille octingentos. Et sic
hic terminatur totum uetus testamentum. Et inc. test. nouum.

The illuminated initials are of very excellent execution, deviating
in the cases marked with an asterisk from the ordinary cycle.

   1. *Exodus.* Three Jews on *L.* Moses on *R.* horned, with tables.
   2. *Levit.* Two Jews hold lambs, one kneels. On *R.* by an altar, Christ. On the
altar are indistinct objects.
   3. *Num.* Moses horned on *L.* with scroll LOCVTV(s). Christ on *R.*

*4. *Deut.* Two Jews, one of them (Joshua) puts the tables of the Law into the Ark, an open red box on four legs. Moses on *R.* directs.

*5. *Jos.* Joshua nimbed, with book. Christ on *R.* with book.

6. *2 Reg.* David seated on *L.* Man about to behead the seated Amalekite.

7. *3 Reg.* David in bed. Courtier and Abishag by him.

8. *4 Reg.* Ahaziah in bed. Elijah with scroll PRELL.

9. *1 Par.* A tall man in *C.*, three on each side.

10. *2 Par.* Solomon kneels. Christ by altar. Building on *R.*

11. *1 Esd.* At top three workmen building. Below, bust of man in window. At bottom Cyrus pointing up.

*12. *Neh.* A man stoning a kneeling nimbed man on *R.* The artist has mistaken Neemias for Jeremias.

*13. *2 Esdr.* Esdras with book.

*14. *3 Esdr.* King on *L.* Falling city on *R.*

*15. *4 Esdr.* Similar. The King puts his hand to his face.

16. *Judith.* Beheading Holofernes in bed.

17. *Esther.* Ahasuerus throned above stretches down his sceptre to Esther below.

18. *Job.* Seated with two friends by him on *R.* His wife on *L.*

19. Psalter. *Gall.* *Beatus uir.* David sits playing harp.

20. „   *Rom.*   „   David sits playing fiddle.

21. *Dominus illuminatio.* *Gall.* David kneels pointing to his eye. Head of Christ above.

22. *Dominus illuminatio.* *Rom.* Samuel on *L.* anoints David. Jesse on *R.*

23. *Dixi custodiam.* *Gall.* Like no. 21. David points to his mouth.

*24. „   *Rom.* David points to his mouth. Green devil on *R.*

25. *Dixit insipiens.* *Gall.* David throned on *L.* Bald fool with club and cake.

26. „   *Rom.* A king (Saul) standing. A sword from a cloud on *R.* behind him pierces his body.

27. *Salvum.* *Gall.* Christ above half-length with orb. David half-length in water below.

28. *Salvum.* *Rom.* Similar. With variations in colour.

29. *Exultate.* *Gall.* David plays on five bells with two hammers.

30. „   *Rom.* David plays on a dulcimer on his lap with two plectra.

31. *Cantate.* *Gall.* Three coped clerks with two books facing *R.*

32. „   *Rom.* Similar. They have one book, and there is an altar on *R.*

33. *Dixit dominus.* *Gall.* Christ throned with orb.

34. „   *Rom.* The Father and Son throned. The Dove between them.

Quid gloriaris and *Ad dominum* have decorative initials.

35. *Prov.* Solomon on *L.* with rod. Rehoboam half-nude with book on *R.*

36. *Jer.* Exactly like no. 12.

37. *Hosea.* Takes Gomer's hand.

38. *Joel.* Seated with scroll UER(BUM).

39. *Amos.* Hooded, feeding sheep, head of Christ in sky.

40. *Obadiah.* Seated with scroll UISIO.

41. *Jonah.* Emerges from fish's mouth. City above.

42. *Micah.* Writes at desk.

43. *Nahum.* Seated with scroll ONUS.

44. *Habakkuk.* Similar.

45. *Zephaniah.* Similar: scroll UER(BUM).
46. *Haggai.* Standing: scroll IN.
47. *Zechariah.* Standing: blank scroll : angel above.
48. *Malachi.* Seated with scroll ONU(S).
49. 1 *Macc.* Mattathias about to behead kneeling apostate Jew with pig's head in dish.
50. 2 *Macc.* Jew gives letter to messenger on *R.*
51. *Matt.* Initial the length of the text. Jesse reclining, two lamps hang above. Out of him proceeds a tree containing five seated kings in elliptical medallions: then the Virgin (?) a beardless figure with book : then Christ with orb.
52. *Mark.* Standing with scroll INICIUM : below, winged lion with scroll MARCUS.
53. *Luke.* Zacharias by wall on *L.* Angel by altar under trefoil arch on *R.*
54. *John.* Standing, with book: above, eagle with scroll.
55. *Acts.* Two groups of Apostles looking up at the feet of the ascending Christ.
56. *James.* Standing, with scroll IACOB(US).
57. 1 *Pet.* Peter seated in blue chasuble and tiara, with key.
58. 2 *Pet.* Peter seated in pink chasuble bareheaded, with book and key.
59. 2 *Joh.* John seated.
60. 3 *Joh.* John seated with scroll SENI(ORI).
61. *Jude.* Standing with scroll IUDAS.
62. *Rom.* Paul with gold cross: a Jew on *R.*
63. 1 *Cor.* Paul holds sheathed sword by the point.
64. 2 *Cor.* With sword and book.
The subsequent Epistles have variations of this subject. Paul seated or standing, or half-length with sword.
65. *Heb.* Jew seated on *L.* Paul with sword seated on *R.*
66. *Apoc.* John seated writing on scroll APOCA(LIPSIS). Church spires above.
Each letter of the Interpretationes has a handsome initial.

II. 1. 8   C. M. A. 133

117. PARLIAMENTARY RECORDS.

Paper, 15⅝ × 10¾, ff. 290 written.   Cent. xvii.

Given by Joshua Barnes, whose book-plate is in the cover. Below it is written :

Bibliothecae ejusdem Collegii dedit. Edwardi Tertii Regis Angliae etc. Historiae Author egregius 1702.

Vellum binding with gold tooling.
On the flyleaf: Joshua Barnes, Coll. Eman.

MS. authenticum a Roberto Cotton milite ex Archiuis collectum: dein ex Bibliotheca Comitis Northamptoniae ad Manus Dⁿⁱ Mich. Payne de Coll. Trin. pervenit opera Dⁿⁱ Compton: et a praedicto D. Mich. Payne dono mihi Datum 16 Martii 168⅞.

Contents :

> Records of Parliaments from 5 Edward II. to 21 Richard II., mostly
> in English.
> The first item is:
>> Ordinances par les Prelates Countes et Barones fits a Londres
>> par l'assent du Roy Edward 2. An°. 5to.
> It is very well written.

II. 1. 9   C. M. A. 44

118. LYRA IN EPISTOLAS.

Paper, with vellum flyleaves, $15\frac{1}{2} \times 11\frac{1}{2}$, ff. 197 + 2, double
columns of 61 lines. Cent. xv (1460), very well written, with pretty
decorative initials.

Ex dono Thome Bell hujus Collegii Socij A. d. 1629.

On the flyleaf :

> Ad Carthusien*ses* prope delf.

A piece is cut out of the leaf below. Above :

> Istud volumen legauit Theodoricus petri de hoern qui obiit a. d. milles. quadringent.
> septuag. tercio, decima die mens. decembr. Ex instructione mag. Joh. roeper de harlim.
> Oretur pro eo prope deum.
> Et continentur in isto vol. Epistole pauli, Epistole canonice, Actus Apostolorum,
> Apocalipsis. At each end. Theodoricus petri de hoern legauit (hunc librum).

Black leather binding, stamped over wooden boards. Title on
fore edge.

> Lyra in Epistolas acta et Apocalypsin.

Collation : 1 flyleaf. 1⁶ (wants 1) 2⁸–25⁸, vellum flyleaf.

Contents :

1. Lyra super Epistolas Pauli . . . . f. 1
   Ecce descripsi eam tibi tripliciter.
2. Idem super Epistolas Canonicas 124
   Quatuor sunt minima terre.
3. Idem super Actus 145
   Repleti sunt omnes spiritu.
4. Idem super Apocalipsin 173
   Oportet te iterum predicare.
   Ends f. 197 *b*: cum omnibus uobis. Amen. Expl. postilla
   super apoc. Nycolai de lyra fratris minorum, doctoris sacre
   theologie.

Postille huius libri supra (?) Epistolas predictas finite sunt Per
Allardi reyneri oriundi filii de Akersloet quondam Custodis
in Velzen et in noirtigherhout manus. a.d. milles. quad-
ringentes. sexages. mense octobris xxxiᵃ die illius mensis s.
in profecto (profesto) omnium sanctorum.

II. 1. 10

119. VALOR BENEFICIORUM.

Paper, 15¾ × 10¼, ff. 6 + 89.   Cent. xvii (1627), very well written.

Contents:

Valor Beneficiorum Angliae et Walliae.
Tabula Angliae . . . . f. i
A fine initial in pen-work in which is written
   Script. Anno Dom. 1627.
Tabula Walliae vi
Comitatus Kancie 1
Additiones 84

II. 1. 11   C. M. A. 123

120. FLORES PSALTERII PER LETHBERTUM.

Paper, 15 × 11, ff. 117, double columns of 59 lines.   Cent. xv
late, neatly written in a foreign hand.

At the end the names Robertus fowberie and Thomas Bywater
1600, the latter probably the donor of the book to the College.
Collation: unintelligible to me.

Contents.

Flores Psalterii.
Beginning imperfectly in Ps. xxxvi. *getur et viam eius uolet.* Nam
  apud se ipsum non inuenit homo nisi errorem et peccatum.
Ends f. 117 *b* on Ps. cl. Et quia separare se a deo mors est *Omnis
  spiritus laudet dominum.* Amen.
Expl. flores psalterii de collectione Lethberti Abbatis Sᶜⁱ Ruphi.
At the bottom of the page (xv, xvi)
    payd to the pawer. } xiˢ viijᵈ.
    for (?) the Scriven*er* (?). }
    Item precium prior a nobyl xxᵈ.

II. I. 12   C. M. A. 20

121. HIERONYMUS SUPER PROPHETAS.

Vellum, $14\frac{1}{2} \times 9\frac{3}{4}$, ff. 183, double columns of 34 lines.   Cent. xii,
in a very beautiful hand, with some interesting initials.   2 fo. gone.
Collation: 1^8 (wants 2) 2^8–23^8.

Contents :

Title in red and green capitals.
Inc. Explanationum in Osee prophetam beati Ieronimi presbiteri
  liber primus ad Pammachium
    Si in explanationibus omnium prophetarum.
Initial in yellow and white on blue ground. Above, Hosea (?)
  beardless seated with scroll. A dove flies toward him from *R.*
  His scroll descends into the lower half of the letter, where it
  forms a book held by a nimbed beardless person on *R.* Jerome
  nimbed, bearded, tonsured, sits on *L.* at desk and turns to touch
  the book. By him is a small table with pens stuck in it, and horn.
Initial to Hosea gone with the second leaf.
Lib. II. f. 19 *l:* qui sepe nauigat.   Initial in green on blue ground.
  A ship with green sail and white cross on mast sailing on brown-
  red sea. Four people are in it, a steerer, one in hat adjusting
  sail, a woman and another man.
Lib. III. f. 49 *b.*
In Johel, f. 60.   Good decorative initial.
In Amos, f. 81.   Good initial.   Lib. II. f. 98.   Lib. III. f. 116 *b.*
  Unfinished initial of curious colouring.
In Abdiam, f. 137 *b,* curious coloured initials.
In Ionam, f. 147 *b.*
In Micheam, f. 164 *b.*   Lib. II. f. 183 ending imperfectly
  maxima in cura illum imitari.
A curious initial to this last book.

II. I. 13, 14, 15

122, 3, 4.

Paper, $13\frac{3}{4} \times 8\frac{3}{4}$.   Three volumes.   Cent. xvii (1692), well written.
Given by Dr Samuel Parr.
On the flyleaf:
25 Jan. 1791.

Mr Francis Hargrave requests Dr Parr's acceptance of the three volumes of the Copy
of Lord Hale's Manuscript entitled "Tentamina de Ortu Natura et Immortalitate
Animae Humanae."
The treatise appears to have been finished 25 July 1673.
Notice of this treatise is taken in Burnett's Life of Lord Hale.

On the title-page :

Bought of Messrs White in Fleet Street and since newly bound. F. H.

Also some directions by Mr Hargrave to the binder, and his signature.

Title : An Essay by Sr Matthew Hale concerning the Soul. Written 1673.

The originall of this Treatise, writt in his owne hand, was copied 1692. It being lent to Sr Robert Southwell by his grandson Matthew Hale of Lincoln's Inn Esqre.

The text is on one side of the leaf only.

Vol. 1. ff. 1–31   contains chapters I.–IX.
Vol. 2.   132–246   ,,   ,,   X.–XVIII.
Vol. 3.   247–439 + 1–10 ,,   ,,   XIX.–XXXIV. and a Prayer.

In Vol. II. is a note by Dr Parr (9 Feb. 1818, Hatton, near Warwick) presenting the MS. to the College, and stating that he had at one time thought of publishing it.

II. 1. 19   C. M. A. 48

125. CHRONICA.

Vellum, 16 × 10¾, ff. 32, 50 lines to a page. Cent. xiv, well written.

Collation : 1^{12} 2^{14} 3^6.

Contents :

Prefacio in opusculum subscriptum s. de gestis anglorum . . f. 1
    Non solum audiendis scripture sacre uerbis.
The compiler names the Gesta Britonum, Bede and Henry of
    Huntingdon as his authorities.
Cronice de gestis ac nominibus regum britonum anglorum saxonum
    danorum et normannorum   2
    Iste brutus ex genere troianus.
The left side of each page is occupied by a pedigree-line with the
    names in circles. On the *R*. margin are sometimes conventional
    drawings of towns, churches and conflagrations.
Some interest seems to be felt by the compiler in Salisbury and in
    the Carthusian houses of Witham and Henton (Hinton): other-
    wise I do not detect any trace of his environment.
Ends with the death of Edward I.
    Qui anno xxxv° regni sui moriens apud westmonast. sepelitur.

II. I. 20   C. M. A. 42

126. PETRI COMESTORIS ALLEGORIAE.

Vellum, 13½ × 9⅝, ff. 36, double columns of 50 lines.   Cent. xiii,
very well written.
Collation : 1¹⁰–3¹⁰ 4⁷ (six left).   2 fo. secundus homo.

Contents :

    Incipiunt allegorie magistri Petri (Comestoris) .   .   .   . f. 1
        In precedentibus premissa descripcione originis.
    Ends imperfectly in Lib. XII. in the section
        De exitu spiritus inmundi ab homine.

On the lower margin of f. 18 *a*, in a hand not much later than
the text, is the name Johannes north'e.

II. 2. 1–14

127–140.

Paper, 12¼ × 8, fourteen volumes.   Cent. xvii.
Given by "Nicolaus Bernard, S.T.D., Coll. Emmanuelis olim
alumnus, Decanus de Drogheda, Domini Protectoris Eleëmosynarius
et in Hospitio Graiensi Concionator Publicus" in 1657.

Matthaei Suttlini Opera.

They consist of treatises against Roman Catholics, e.g. Suarez,
Bellarmine, Gretser, in Latin.
Vols. XI–XIV are in English.   Rejoinder to Kellison's new
Reply etc.

II. 2. 15

Printed.   Sir W. Mildmay's copy of Homer, Basle, 1535.

II. 2. 16
141.

Cicero de Oratore, printed, interleaved with notes by William Bennett, Bp of Cloyne, 1794–1820.

II. 2. 17   C. M. A. 118
142. Concilium Basileense.

Paper, 12 × 8½, ff. 198, various numbers of lines to a page. Cent. xv.

Ex dono Rodolphi Cudworth.

From Norwich Cathedral Priory. On f. 1 is Liber Johannis Stowe monachi.... Bale (*Index Scriptorum* p. 258 ed. Poole and Bateson) has a notice of John Stowe in these words:

> Jo. Stowe monachus Norwicensis scripsit
> Acta Concilii Basiliensis li. 1.   Sacrosancte generali synodo Basiliensi.
> Item collectiones varias li. 1.
>   Et in illis habentur scripta Adami Eston Cardinalis.
> Item scripsit actus suos scolasticos li. 1.   In solio residens eminenti gratia Benedictus etc.
> *Ex museo Roberti Talbot.*

The first *incipit* here is that of the first tract in this MS. The other is found on f. 107. This MS., then, belonged to R. Talbot and is that seen by Bale.

Collation: 1 flyleaf.   1¹² 2¹² (+ 1) 3¹² 4¹⁶ 5⁶ (+ 1) | 6⁶ | 7¹⁴ (10–12 canc.) | 8⁴ | 9⁷ (eleven) | 10¹² | 11⁷ (seven) 12⁴ 13⁴ 14⁶ 15⁴ (+ slip) 16⁴ 17² 18² 19⁷ (one) 20⁷ 21⁷ (eight in all) 22⁸ 23⁶ 24⁷ (nine) 25¹² 26⁷ (sixteen).   The greater part of the volume consists of miscellaneous papers bound together.   I have relied largely on the numbering of the quires, made by a binder perhaps early in cent. xix.

On f. 1 (the flyleaf) in large letters

> Tractatus domini patria(rche) anthiocheni

and some notes.

On f. 2 a note, perhaps by Talbot:

> Tractatus iste nititur probare (quod concilium) generale legitime congregatum sit supra Papam (?).

Contents :

E. C. C.   8

In opido Bern alias Verona Pragensis dioc.   A miracle of the
Host and a Hussite priest.
Articuli oblati concilio ex parte Regni bohemie et Marchionatus
Moravie etc. a.d. m.cccc.xxxiii, in festo Tiburcii post laurencii f. 169
13. Part of a book like the Rosarium Theologiae (alphabetical) . 171
Abstinencia precepit deus ade.   Ends in *Paupertas.*
14. List of certain articles divided into conclusions, whereof the
exposition follows.   The list begins
Virtus moralis que per actus adquiritur 183
Prehonorabiles domini quodam prouerbiali edicto   .   . 183 *b*
Ends f. 198 with a second copy of f. 183 *a*.

II. 2. 18   C. M. A. 16

143. GREGORIUS IN EZECHIELEM.

Vellum, 12½ × 7⅞, ff. 130 + 1, 35 lines to a page. Cent. xii
early, in a very beautiful hand, rather round.   Initials often in
purple.   2 fo. a cogitationibus.
Written for a monastery dedicated to St Germanus, probably
Selby.

Given by Tho. Bywater.

Collation: 1 flyleaf.   1⁸ 2¹² 3¹² 4⁸–11⁸ 12¹⁰ 13⁸–15⁸.

Contents :

1. Gregorius in Ezechielem (LXXVI. 785).
On flyleaf in red capitals (near the bottom)
Inc. epistola b. Gregorii (papae erased) ad Marianum
episcopum.
Heading in green and red capitals, a third line (containing such
words as episcopus or papa urbis Romae) scratched out.
Dilectissimo patri Mariano Episcopo Gregorius Omelias que in
beato hezechiel.
Expl. epistola.   Inc. omelia prima.
Dei omnipotentis aspiratione.
Initial with green, blue and red ground, on it a gryphon in white.
Hom. xxii ends f. 127 *b* : ad hereditatem perpetuam erudit. Sit
itaque gloria...deus per omnia sec. sec. Amen.
2. Verses in the same hand   .   .   .   . f. 128
Tu miserere mei pater inclite sancte sacerdos,
Iudicis aduentu tu miserere mei.
Gracia multa datur te complacante tonantem.
Inplicitisque tuis gracia multa datur.
Omnibus alme tuis famulis GERMANE faueto.
Condescende pius omnibus alme tuis.

Laudibus omnimodis chorus hic tua mira frequentat,
Te uenerande colens laudibus omnimodis.
Optineas ueniam cunctis erratibus orat.
     ? diu
Utque de*u*m (!) uiuat optineas ueniam.
Suscipe sancte pater quem librum te duce scripsi,
Munera parua licet suscipe sancte pater.
Consonet omnis amen chorus hic domino benedicens,
Te quoque magnificans consonet omnis AMHN.

3. Notes on the Holy Land, in a different but hardly later hand . f. 128
Ab occidente est introitus iherusalem per portam dauid. Intra
ciuitatem est sepulchrum domini. Foris in capite ipsius est
medium mundi etc.
Ends: Idus iulii introitus ierusalem sancte ciuitatis quando (?)
dominus liberauit de manibus paganorum et tradidit in
manibus Christianorum. Eodem die diuisio apostolorum.

4. (T)etbaldus stampensis ad Robertum lincolniensem Ep. de
quibusdam in diuina pagina titubantibus et plane contra
claues ecclesie predicantibus. (See Dachery, *Spicil.* III. 445)   129
Si quis et predicando temere diffiniat aliquem non posse saluari
quacunque hora manus suas penitentie dederit fallitur etc. .   129
This is in a curious hand (of cent. xiii), very black and rather
irregular. Names of popes scratched out.
Ends 130 *b*: comminutus in puluerem redigatur.
In a hand of cent. xvi:
    forma cristi (?) imitetus (?).
...consider y^t we are all subiect and under the mightie hand
of God etc.
Also
    Author refertissimus diuinis speculationibus 1641.

II. 2. 19

144. BIBLIA.

Vellum, 11¾ × 9⅛, ff. 436 + 5, double columns of 51 lines.
Cent. xiv, clearly and well written.

On f. 401 *b*:

Iste liber est Carth*usiensium* prope Magunc. et hoc fuit scriptum a° m° ccc°xciii
crastina concepcionis virginis marie.

At the end (twice)

    Iste est liber Carthusiensium prope Magunciam.

From this Carthusian house of Mainz many of Laud's MSS.
and of the Arundel MSS. in the British Museum came.

At the end is also :

Ego Walcherus laynstein de hedderspach vicarius in ecclesia Mag(untinensi) accomodaui hunc librum biblie a Cartusien. prope Magunciam in die S. Mauricii a.d. m°. cccc°. xx°.

Old binding, yellow skin over boards, incised lines.   Clasps gone : trace of chain staple below lower clasp on 1st cover.

Collation : a⁶ (1 stuck to cover, 6 canc., + a slip) 1⁸ 2⁸ 3¹²–33¹² 34⁸ 35⁶ | 36¹² 37¹² 38¹⁰ (10 stuck to cover).

Contents:

f. 1 (stuck to cover) had a list of the books on it of which the end only is visible.

Inc. tabula ewangeliorum et epistolarum dominicalium per totum annum . . . . f. ii

De libris incipiendis et legendis tam in choro quam in refectorio sequitur ordo talis . . . . 18 b

Post octauam Penthecostes die quacunque trium leccionum occurrente libros regum incipimus.

In hac presenti biblia continentur hii infrascripti libri secundum ordinem secularium et non secundum ordinem nostrum s. Carthus.

List of the books follows.

Throughout the volume are notes in a later hand of these preliminary leaves, showing the order of the books for reading purposes.

Jerome's prologues.   Frater Ambrosius.
                        Desiderii mei.

Genesis—2 Chron.

Oratio Manase filii Ezechie.

1–3 Esdras, Tob., Judith, Esther, Job.

Gallican Psalter.

Prov., Ecclus.   Oratio Salomonis.

Isa.—Mal.

1, 2 Macc. Expl. lib. secundus mach. versus habens mille octin-gentos.   A blank leaf.

Prologues to Gospels.   Matheus cum primum.
                          Plures fuisse.
                          Beatissimo pape.
                          Matheus ex iudeis.

Evv.

Prologues to Epp.   Epistole pauli ad romanos
                      Omnis textus.
                      Primum queritur.
                      Romani sunt qui.
                      Romani sunt in partibus.

There has been a mistake at the end of Philippians.   The scribe seems to have gone from Phil. to 1 Thess. omitting Colossians,

and to have inserted Col. before 1 Tim. This has been rectified
by crossings out and patchings, perhaps not worth describing
in detail.

Acts, Epp. Cath., Apoc., ending f. 402.   402 *b* blank.

Interpretationes nominum. Aaz—Zuzim .   .   .   .   . f. 403

  Laus patri domino proli cum pneumate sancto.

The ordinary prologues to the books occur in their places.
The ornament consists of blue and red flourished initials well
executed, with an occasional dragon or grotesque.

II. 3. 1, 2
145, 6.

Printed.   Barnes's Homer with some autograph notes.

II. 3. 3
147. (BARNESII) PRAELECTIONES MISCELLANEAE.

II. 3. 4, 5
148, 9. BARNESII PRAELECTIONES IN SOPHOCLEM.

II. 3. 6
150. EIUSDEM PRAELECTIONES IN ODYSSEAM.

II. 3. 7
151. EIUSDEM PRAELECTIONES IN PINDARUM.

II. 3. 8, 9
152, 3. EIUSDEM PRAELECTIONES ECCLESIASTICAE.

(Divinity Lectures in Emmanuel Chappel) 1685–90.

II. 3. 10
154. PRAELECTIONES ECCLESIASTICAE ET IN HOMERUM.

II. 3. 11

155. RICHARDSONI PRAELECTIONES ECCLESIASTICAE.

By J. Richardson, Regius Professor of Divinity, 1607–1617.

II. 3. 12

156.

A further series of the same, in modern binding.

II. 3. 13–15

157–9.

Printed.   Latin Bible interleaved, with notes by Henry Hubbard.

II. 3. 16, 17

160, 1.

Printed.   Greek Testament (1674) interleaved, with notes by Henry Hubbard.

II. 3. 18, 19

162, 3.

Printed.   Electra of Sophocles interleaved, with notes by Bp Bennet.

II. 3. 20, 21

164, 5.

Printed.   Greek Testament (1756) interleaved, with notes by the same.

II. 3. 22

166.

Longinus de Sublimitate (ed. Pearce 1773) interleaved, with notes by the same.

II. 3. 23
167.

Cicero de Oratore lib. I. interleaved, with notes by the same. Read in the Lecture Room of Emmanuel College in 1786. Given by Bp Bennet.

II. 3. 25
168.

Taciti Germania et Agricola (1788) interleaved, with notes by the same.

III. I. 1–12
169-180.

Manuscripts by Joshua Barnes, viz.

III. I. 1
169.

Portfolio of Miscellaneous Papers, some in English, including:

A second voyage to Granta.
An Elegy on the death of his grace James Duke of Ormond etc.

Mostly on classical subjects.

III. I. 2
170.

Landgartha or the Amazon Queen of Denmark and Norwey. An Entertainment Design'd for their Royal Highnesses the Prince and Princess of Denmark.
Notes on the Anacreontica.

III. I. 3
171.

A folio volume written at both ends containing Latin and English poems by Joshua Barnes.

III. 1. 4
172.

Plays by Joshua Barnes, in English :

1. The Academie or the Cambridge Dunns (2 copies).
2. Engelbert, an opera and tragedy.

Two copies of a Discourse on the Art of War called "the Christian Soldier" or "the English Soldier." Another English play without title.

III. 1. 5
173.

Lexicon Latino-Graecum (A–I).

III. 1. 6
174.

Version in Greek metre of Psalms i–xli.
Private accounts.
Fragments in Greek and English, and some drafts of letters.

III. 1. 7
175.

Franciados Libri I–VIII.
Common-place book.   Tract on Greek accents.
Miscellaneous notes.

III. 1. 8
176.

English Poems.

Κοσμοποιΐα.
Man's Fall.
Φιλανθρωπία.
A Hymn.
An Eclogue etc.

III. I. 9
177.

English Poems :
    Hengist.
    A Persian Phancy (?).

III. I. 10
178.

Greek Poems (with Latin versions) :
    Esthera.
    Josephus.
    Metaphrases.
    Bellum Anglo-Belgicum seu Mors Nobilissimi Comitis Sandavici.

III. I. 11
179.

Directions and advice to Students.   ff. 123 in English.

III. I. 12
180.

Lexicon Latino-Graecum, complete.

III. I. 13
181. MISCELLANEOUS PAPERS.

Paper, $11\frac{3}{4} \times 7\frac{3}{4}$, ff. circ. 250, several volumes.   Cent. xvi, xvii.
Table of contents by Dr Farmer.

    I.   A discourse written by the Earle of Devonshire in defence
         of his marriage wth the Lady Rich.
    II. An English version of three books of Seneca *de Ira*.   With
         a rough initial containing the arms of England and E.R.
    III. The objection to Sir J. Hamilton's Title to certain lands,
         and the opinion of Mr Humfr. Davenport (1625).
         The proposicion on the behalfe of the Lo. Abp. of Canterbury
         (Bancroft) concerning prohibitions granted out of the
         Court of Common Pleas.

    V. To Mr Anthony Bacon.

        An apoligie of the Earle of Essex against those wch falslie and maliciouslie take him to be the only hinderance of the peace and quyet of his Cuntre.

   VI. (A note from W. Warren Ashford, 30 Jul. 1710, accompanying the MS. next following, which is presented to the College by Mr Halford, Curate of Great Chart.)

        Bp Bedell's defence of the Answer to Mr Alablaster's fower demandes against a treatise intituled

        The Catholics Reply upon Bedell's Answere to Mr Alablaster's foure demandes. (Another copy is in MS. Lambeth 772.)

  VII. A few leaves of notes and extracts apparently in the hand of III. 1. 14.

        Two leaves headed, Recusancy of Communion with the Church of England, containing Distinctions and Texts besides.

 VIII. In the hand of III. 1. 14.

        Doubts proposed against some passages of the Doctrine of Predestination.

        Discourse of Mr John Cotton touchinge the time when the Lordes Day beginneth.

        Answer by Mr Wheatly.

        Concerninge Usurye by Mr John Cotton.

        Anatomy of a Christian.

        The doctrine of the Saints perseverance. At end, Reinoldes.

        A tract signed Saunderson :

            All the decrees of God are eternall.

        A breife and pithy catechisme as it was deliuered in Emanuell College Chappell 1628, per Anth. Tukneye.

        The Lordes Prayer briefly explained.

        A table containinge the summe of Theologie by Dr Preston M^r of Em. Col.

        Mr Richerson his Catechisme.

        A Catechisme by Mr Hopkins: in double columns.

        Of Catechisinge.

        That the lawe is to be taught before ye gospels.

        Sermons by Bishop Andrewes (seven in number).

III. 1. 14
182.

Paper, 12 × 8, ff. circ. 100.   Cent. xvii, well written.

An anonymous Theological treatise or collection of treatises, ending with a long exposition of the Ten Commandments.

    It begins

        Clemens Alexandrinus writing of instruction or catechising in his three books.

III. 1. 15
183.

Paper, 12 × 8, ff. 45.   Cent. xvii.

Given by Joshua Barnes.   A note by him.   " This printed in Quarto and Octavo both An°. 1641."

The Epistle dedicated to Mr E. M. in Graies Inne in London.
Dear and louinge frende I have receaued about x daies since.
Imperfect: the signature gone.
Text: Not longe before this laste Christmas I was requested by a letter.

III. 1. 16
184.

Papers, 12¾ × 8, and larger folding sheets.   Cent. xviii.

Papers on Dr Bentley's Case, viz.
Responsum Cancellarii, Magistrorum et Scholarium Uniuersitatis Cantabr. ad Breue domini Regis huic schedule annexat'.
Notes upon the Argument in relation to the returne made by the University of Cambridge to the Mandamus issued by the Court of Kings Bench for restoring Richard Bentley to his Degrees.
Arguments of Mr Reeve and Sᵣ Philip Yorke in the same case.

III. 1. 17
185.   LATIN PLAYS.

Paper, 12¼ × 8, ff. circ. 80.   Cent. xvii, neatly written.

1. Scyros. Fabula pastoralis acta coram Principe Charolo et
     Comite Palatino Mens. Mart. 30, an°. 1612.
   Authore Dʳᵉ Brooks Coll. Trin.
   Letter of James I to the University. Gratulatur academiae de
     beneficio collato in negando oppidanis jus Ciuitatis. 4 kal.
     Mai. 1616.
   Letter of the University to James (per Mag. Aegid. Fletcher).
     4 Feb. 1616.
2. Zelotypus.
   Oratio funebris on John Gostling.
   Letter of the University to Charles I.
   To the Chancellor Id. Jun. 1626.

3. Euribates.
    Authore M. Cruso Caii Coll.
    Signed Thom. Holbech.
    Oratio funebris on Sir Thomas Bodley.
4. Roxana.   Authore D^{ct} Alablaster Coll. quondam Trin. Socio.
5. Clytophon.
    Al. Gul. Bretonus possessor. Gul. Ainseworthus scriptor.
6. Fraus Honesta (by Stubbe of Trinity: printed 1632).
    Signed W.B.

III. 1. 18
186.

Paper, 13⅛ × 8½ (and smaller), ff. 81, written on one side.
Cent. xviii (1710, 11), by Joshua Barnes.

Ἐξήγησις Ἰωάννου Γραμματικοῦ τοῦ Τζέτζου εἰς τὴν Ὁμήρου Ἰλιάδα.

Transcribed from the MS. belonging to John Moore Bp of Norwich, later of Ely, by
Joshua Barnes 'quando Homeri editionem faceret An⁰. 1710, 1711.'
Moore's MS. is now at Trinity College, R. 16. 33.

III. 1. 19
187.

Paper, 11⅝ × 8, ff. 85.   Cent. xvi.

A Tariye (Terrier) booke of the landes of Sr John Gascoyn, knight, lying in
Cardington etc. in ye Countie of Bedford.

The date is 6 Edward VI.

III. 1. 20
188.

Paper, 11½ × 7½, ff. 28.   Cent. xvii early, well written.

Catalogue of a Library in Latin, seemingly all of printed books.

The press-marks are of this form.

In classe 11^a ex plaga boreali (or australi).

There are at least 17 classes on the north side, and at least
12 on the south.

III. I. 21
189.

Paper, 8⅜ × 6⅜, ff. 17.   Cent. xvii, very clearly written.

Thomae Gatakeri Praeloquium ad M. Antonini editionem scriptum propria manu.
Dedit Tho. Dilingham, A.M. huius Collegii, Bibliothecae Collegii Emmanuelis
A.D. 1695.

Note by Dr Farmer.   " It was printed from this copy."

III. I. 22
190.

Paper, 6 × 3¾, ff. 44.   Cent. xvii, very probably from Sancroft.

A Direction to be observed by N.N. if hee meane to proceede in answering the booke
intituled Mercy and Truth or Charity mayntayned by Catholicks.

III. I. 23
191.

Paper, 7⅝ × 5⅞, ff. 10.   Cent. xvii, ill written.
Endorsed :

P.G. letter to J.B. aboute officiatinge in Publique.   1652.

III. I. 24
192.

Paper, 5⅞ × 3½.   Cent. xviii.

A printed copy of the Anacreon Christianus of Joshua Barnes,
Cambridge, 1703, with some additional poems in Greek and Latin
in the author's hand, viz. on King Charles's Oak, a Hymn to the
Trinity, a Prayer, Ps. liii, lxxxvii, cxxxiv, and another beginning

Φύσις κέρατα ταύροις.

III. I. 25–27
193–195.

Lectures on Optics, Mechanics, Astronomy, by Hubbard.
Cent. xviii.   4to.

III. 1. 28, 29
196, 197.

Lectures on Logic by Bp Bennet.

III. 1. 30
198.

Notes on St Luke's Gospel.

III. 1. 31
199.

Notes on the Greek Theatre and the *Electra* of Sophocles.

III. 1. 32
200.

Paper, 9¼ × 7⅜, ff. circ. 150 written.   Cent. xviii late.
1. Notes on Herodotus.
2. Notes on Tacitus (at the other end of the volume).

? By Bishop Bennet.

III. 1. 33
201.

Paper, 8 × 6½, pp. 280.   Cent. xviii late.
Ex Libris Ric. Hardy Coll. Eman. Cantab. 1704.

A mathematical Note-Book.

III. 1. 34
202.

Paper, 7¾ × 6¼, pp. 239.   Cent. xviii.
On p. 1 : T. E. Marshall, Emm. Coll. 1833.

Observationes Philologicae in Actus Apostolorum haustae ex ore viri Cl. necnon Doctissimi L. C. Valkenarii.

They extend to ch. xx. 35.   The name of the writer is cut out at the end.

III. I. 35
203.

Paper, 8¾ × 7½, ff. circ. 100.   Cent. xviii late.

1. Notes on Juvenal.
2. (At the other end) Notes on the *Germania* of Tacitus.

? By Bishop Bennet.

III. I. 36–40
204–208.

Manuscripts in the autograph of the Rev. T. S. Hughes, B.D., Fellow of Emmanuel College, and Christian Advocate 1822–1829.

They were presented by the author to J. Lee of Doctors Commons and Colworth in 1828.   In 1889 Dr Christian D. Ginsburg presented them to the Bishop of Winchester.

They were afterwards presented by W. Aldis Wright, M.A., Vice-master of Trinity College, to Emmanuel College.

Mr Hughes's principal work was *Travels in Sicily, Greece and Albania*, London, 1820.

III. I. 36
204.

Folio.   Remarks on the Turkish or Ottoman Empire.

III. I. 37
205.

Quarto.   Letter to the *Times* on Parga (1826 May) signed, A Grecian Traveller.

III. I. 38
206.

Quarto.   Belshazzar's Feast.   A Poem.

III. 1. 39
207.

Quarto. Notes on Belshazzar's Feast.

III. 1. 40
208. Octavo inlaid in a Quarto Book.

The Doctrine of St Paul with regard to the Divine Nature of
Jesus Christ considered: more particularly in answer to a pamphlet
by B. Mardon, M.A. entitled: "The Apostle Paul an Unitarian;
especially as appears from a minute examination of the celebrated
passage in his Ep. to the Philippians ii. 6–11 etc."
Printed by Newby, Cambridge, 1827.

III. 1. 41
209.

Paper, 7⅞ × 6, ff. 32, 24 lines to a page. Cent. xvii, well written.
Belonged to the Rev. Dr B. Bandinel (New College, Oxford).
There is a note of its being borrowed from him by P. B(liss)
Registrar of the University of Oxford. In 1838 he gave it to
H. Cotton, who notes that his "father the Rev. James Bandinel
purchased it in Ireland while residing there as Chaplain to the
Marquess of Buckingham, Lord Lieutenant."
Another note by Mr Cotton says:

Mem: Malone's MS. 8, a collation of the printed copy with a MS. in the Bodleian
Library made by Malone. The readings of that MS. vary slightly from this. Mem: to
give the variation.

Contents:

The Shepheards Tale of yᵉ Powder plot.
By the Right Reverend William Bedell late Bp of Kilmore in
Ireland.
In authorem.
Willy thy rimes so sweetly runne and rise.
Ends p. 32
Faire fall ye, gentle Shepheard, for your Tale.

Dr Dillingham (Master 1653–1662) possessed a MS. (probably
this) of the poem, from which it was first printed in 1713.
See Dr Shuckburgh, *Two Lives of Bishop Bedell*, 1903.

III. 2. 1–18

210–227. ORIENTAL MANUSCRIPTS.

III. 2. 19

228. BENNETT'S ROMAN ROADS.

Paper, 9⅜ × 7¾, pp. circ. 350.   Cent. xviii, in various hands.
On the flyleaf:

> I beg this MS. book may be deliverd at my death to the Master and Fellows of Emanuel College, Cambridge, for the use of their Library.
>   Wᵐ Cloyne.

This was William Bennett (1745–1820), Bp of Cloyne 1794–1820.

Contents :

> A survey of the Roman Roads in Britain. It begins with a transcript of the *Itinera* of (Pseudo-) Richard of Cirencester, and those in the Antonine Itinerary. Then follows a survey of the roads now traceable, drawn from printed sources and from the personal observation of various persons whose names are attached to each, e.g. Mr Leman, Mr Iremonger etc.
> There is a full Index at the end.
> The MS. was not delivered to the College in accordance with its author's wish: at the end is an extract from a Sale Catalogue of Messrs Puttick and Simpson (Ap. 1, 1896).

III. 2. 20–22.   Printed Books.

III. 2. 23

229. FORMA CONFESSIONIS GENERALIS.

Roll, vellum, 4⅜ broad, by 19 ft. long, consisting of seven skins. Cent. xvi, very neatly written.

Given by Abp Sancroft, according to the MS. Catalogue III. 3. 32.
At the end :

> A copye of an ancient manuscript wᶜʰ as is sayd was Sʳ George Saintpolls and afterwards was Mr Lynolds, Rector of Healyng in Com. Lincoln, and by him gyven to Mʳ John Barnard one of the Fellows of Lincoln Colledge in Oxford, to the end it might remayne in the Lybrary of that Colledge[1].
> Transcribed by me Wilfrid Smith.

[1] No such manuscript is listed in Coxe's Catalogue as being now at Lincoln College.

Headed :

Forma Confessionis Generalis cuiusdam Deuote.

Benedict' pater.   Christe etc.   Confiteor deo et b. Marie etc.

—maxima culpa.   I a very synner knalegyth my sell culpable and gylty unto my lord god my maker etc.

The text, which is in English (northern forms occurring), is divided into heads.

Obedience.   The Ten Commandments.

Continence.   The Seven Sins.

Wilfull pouertt.

The vii workys of mercy.

The v wyttys.

The vii sacraments.

The vii gyfts of ye holy gost.

The vii warkys of mercy gostely.

The iiii cardynall vertues.

Y^e xii artycll.

Ends: and I aske him mercy and forgyfnes.

ffinis.

III. 2. 24

230. Episcopal Offices.

Roll, vellum, 7 in. broad by 8 ft. 6¾ in. long, on six skins. Cent. xiv early, in two very fine large hands. The chief hand closely resembles that of the roll at Canterbury on which the verses of the windows are written.

At top.   W. Sancroft.

It is written from both ends :

A.   1. *Ad pueros confirmandos.*   Adiutorium nostrum in nomine domini etc.

    2. *Ad patenam consecrandam.*

    3. *Ad calicem benedicendum.*

On the back of this in another and rather larger hand is

Forma Sarum ecclesie.

    (*a*) For Confirmation.

    (*b*) Benedictio lintheam*inis.*

    (*c*) Benedictio Corporalis.   This last is finished on the *recto.*

B.   (From the other end.)   Headed with a small *a.*

    1. *Ad clericum faciendum.*

    2. *Benedictio uestimentorum sacerdotalium seu leuiticorum.*

    3. *Benedictio corporalium.*

I have not heard of other rolls resembling this, which was no doubt intended to be held up before the Bishop while the offices were being performed.

III. 2. 25
231. CHRONICLE ROLL.

Roll, vellum, 11⅜ in. broad by 14 ft. 10 in. long, on nine? skins. Cent. xv, very well written, with some good ornament at the top. From Abp Sancroft. At top is the name W. Cant, and a very neat label: Roger Albon sive Albani progenies Regum Angliae ab Adamo ad Henricum sextum lat. Num. 97.

> Prologue: Considerans cronicorum prolixitatem
>> —et ab illo (Bruto) usque ad henricum sextum originaliter finem perduxi.
> Text. Adam in agro damasceno formatus.
> Goes down to Edward IV. Nothing is said of Henry VI except Henricus sextus filius henrici quinti.
> Edward IV ends: de iure tanquam hereditarium a.d. m°. cccc°. lxi°.
> The pedigree occupies the centre. Text on each side.

III. 2. 26
232. CHRONICLE ROLL.

Roll, vellum, 10½ in. broad by 13 ft. 1 in. long, on six skins. Cent. xiii late, very well written. In the initial a shield barry of six *argent* and *azure*: on a bend dexter *gules* three birds displayed *or*.
Given by Abp Sancroft.
Written on both sides:

> A (recto) Compendium Historiarum (in blue capitals).
>> Considerans historie sacre prolixitatem
>>> —usque ad christum finem secundum ordinem nostrum perduxi.
>> Adam in agro damasceno formatus.
>> The table ends with *Christus passus* and a diagram of Christ and the Apostles.
>> Text ends with the call of Matthias.
>> Mathias loco iude etc. inter dies ascensionis et pentecostes.
> B (verso) in another, hardly later, hand.
>> Diagram of the Heptarchy with text in French. Then:
>>> Par cest figur desus escrit peot lem sauer les diuers regnes que furent iadis en engleter. etc.
>> There is a special note that Ricard qui fut roy de allemayne funda le abbaye de hales tut a ses coustages e la est il enterre e dam sienche sa femme reyne de alemayne etc.
>> The pedigree ends with Edward I:
>>> Le Roy Edward le fiz le Roy henry regna (blank).
>> Text ends with Henry III: e il funda la bele eglise de Westmostre tot a ses coustages.

III. 2. 27.   Printed Book.

III. 2. 28

233.

Vellum sheet about 22 in. broad by 19, containing

The Address of Harvard College to Emmanuel College.   Latin, dated 7 Kal.
Dec. 1886.

III. 3. 1

234. JOHN SCOT: FOUNDATION OF THE UNIVERSITIE.

Paper, 12 × 7⅝, ff. 28 written, 35 lines to a page.   Cent. xvii
(1617), very well written and ornamented.
Brown leather binding with gold tooling.
Given by Laurence Chaderton, D.D., Master.

Contents :

The foundation of the Universitie of Cambridge, with a catalogue
of the principall founders and speciall Benefactours of the
Colledges, publike Schooles, and Librarie nowe in the same.
And the names of all the present masters and fellowes of every
perticular Colledge.

Together with the number of Magistrats, Gouernours and Officers
therunto belonging; and the totall number of Students nowe
therin being.

Collected Anno Domini 1617.

Two stanzas of English Verse   .   .   .   . f. 28

(*a*) The age of her that hath outliu'd so many.

(*b*) To the generous Reader.

I write not this to please the braine of him.

Other copies of this book are to be found at Pembroke, King's (2), and Sidney Sussex Colleges.

III. 3. 2

235. GRAMMATICA HEBRAICA.

Paper, $11\frac{3}{8} \times 7\frac{1}{2}$, ff. circ. 180.   Cent. xvi, xvii, well written. On the flyleaf:

> Thomas Kent.
> Will. Quadrin.
> Ex dono Edwardi Greene.

Contents :

> Notes on Hebrew Grammar. § 1 De Consonantibus.
> At 137 *b* begins a list of words and phrases continuing to f. 153 *b*.
> This is followed by some notes on Libb. I, II of the Ethics, written
>   the reverse way.
> At the end a section, De mensibus Hebraeorum.

There are a good many blank leaves.

III. 3. 3

236. FRAGMENTS.

Vellum, of various sizes, bound in a vellum of cent. xviii?

I. $10\frac{1}{2} \times 6\frac{3}{4}$, 36 lines to a page.   Cent. xiv, well written in a charter hand.   Torn, and tender from damp.   ff. 18.

Collation : $1^?$ (1 left) 2^4 3^6 (wants 6) 4^8.

> Fragment of a Cartulary of lands held by William Goscelyn in
>   Snettisham, Norfolk.
> f. 5 is headed Ingalsthorp'.
> The latest date that I can find is 14 Edw. III.

II.   ff. 2, $8 \times 6\frac{1}{8}$, 23 lines to a page.   Cent. xiii?

> A fragment of a Greek service-book containing anthems etc. beginning
>   ἐπὶ σταυροῦ ἀναρτηθεὶς ἑκουσίως χριστέ.

III. ff. 2, 10¾ × 7, 34–5 lines to a page. Cent. xi? in a good small hand.

A fragment of a Greek service-book beginning with a lesson from Gen. xxii. (9–18) τόπον ὃν εἶπεν αὐτῷ ὁ θεός —ὑπήκουσας τῆς ἐμῆς φωνῆς. Followed by one from Prov. xvii. 17 Ἀδελφοὶ· ἐν ἀνάγκαις χρίσιμοι ἔστωσαν· τούτου γὰρ χάριν. The last page is much obliterated.

IV. ff. 12, 11⅜ × 7⅜, 29 lines to a page. Cent. xi? in a fine bold minuscule hanging from lines ruled with a dry point. Headings in semi-uncials. Two quires of six leaves. Fragment of a Greek Metaphrast containing

1. End of a life (little more than the doxology).
2. θαῦμα γενόμενον ὑπὸ τῶν ἁγίων ὁμολογητῶν Γουρία Σαμωνᾶ καὶ Ἀβίβου, imperfect . . . . f. 1
   Νῦν καιρὸς μετὰ τοῦ πνευματοφόρου.
3. End of the life of Nicetas Gothus (?) 7
4. Τοῦ ἐν ἁγ. πατρὸς ἡμῶν Γρηγορίου τοῦ θεολόγου ἐπισκόπου Ναζιανζοῦ λόγος εἰς τὴν χριστοῦ γέννησιν . . . . 9 b
   Χριστὸς γεννᾶται.
   = Hom. 38, ending in § 9, αἵ τε ὑπ' αὐτὸν ἀπο(στατικαὶ δυνάμεις).

V. A quire of four leaves bound in this order—1, 4, 2, 3: 11⅜ × 8, double columns of 26 lines. Cent. xii? well written. Fragments of two orations of S. John Chrysostom, viz.

1. Hom. ad populum Antioch. X. 5—fin.
   Φέρε ἐπὶ τὴν γλυκεῖαν (II. 117 Migne).
2. (Heading in red.) Hom. XI.
   Ἐπειδὰν ἐννοήσω—
   ἐπιτήδειον ζητεῖν χρὴ (110 Migne).

VI. ff. 11, all pairs of leaves except 7 which is single: 11⅜ × 8¼, double columns of 35 lines. Cent. xii? well written: the letters hanging from ruled lines. Fragment of a Metaphrast in Greek for January, containing

1. End of the Translation of the relics of S. John Chrysostom (27 Jan.).
   Nearly two leaves.
2. Βίος καὶ πολιτεία τοῦ ὁσίου πατρὸς ἡμῶν Ἐφραὶμ τοῦ Cυροῦ.
   Ἐφραὶμ ὁ θαυμάσιος (28 Jan.).
   About five leaves.

3. Βίος καὶ μαρτύριον τῶν ἀγ. κ. θαυματουργῶν ἀββᾶ Κύρου κ.
    Ἰωάννου (31 Jan.).
    2½ leaves. Imperfect at end.
    Κύρος ὁ περιφανής.
4. A single leaf relating to Σενούφιος (Senuti).

The leaves are entirely out of order : they should form a quire
of 8 leaves followed by another fragment, of which the first two
and the last leaves remain. Nos. 3–7 gone.

VII. A single leaf, 11¼ × 8½ (originally larger): double columns
of 41 lines. Cent. ix, x, in a very early type of minuscule.
It is bound in the wrong way about: the verso should be
the recto.
It is a leaf of a Greek Bible containing

    Isaiah lix. 4. (κρίσις ἀλη)θηνη· πεποίθασιν ἐπὶ ματαίοις,
    to lx. 11. καὶ ἀνοιχθήσονται αἱ πύλαι σ(ου).

Dr Hort, who has identified this and several other of the
fragments in this volume, remarks: "The readings agree remarkably
with those of 62 of Parsons, a New College (Oxford) MS. of the
Prophets."

III. 3. 4   C. M. A. ? vac.

237. PSEUDO-CHRYSOSTOMI OPUS IMPERFECTUM ETC.

Vellum, 11⅛ × 7⅜, ff. 205, 42 lines to a page. Cent. xiv late, in
more than one ugly hand.
On f. 12 b is

Liber Ricardi pytt ex dono domini Johannis Thornton quondam capellani conducti
in collegio Whytyngton (xvi early).

Collation : 1¹²–17¹² (+ 1).

Contents :

1. Tabula omeliarum S. Crisostomi in imperfecto. Inc. numerus
    et ordo omeliarum S. Crisostomi in imperfecto cum sententiis
    notabilibus in eis contentis .   .   .   . f.   1
    In double columns.
2. Hugo (de S. Victore) de arra anime   5
    Loquar secreto
        —totis uiribus concupisco. Expl. hugo de a. a.
3. Miscellaneous extracts   11
    from Hugo de archa noe, Rabanus, Anselm etc.

4. (Opus imperfectum in Matthaeum) .   .   .   .   .   . f. 13
    Crisostomus primo presbiter Antiochenus postea Archiep.
    CPolitanus omelia prima.
    Sicut referunt matheum
        —stantem in loco sancto.   Amen.
    Expl. omelie Joh. Crisost. patriarche CPol. super matheum
    operis imperfecti.
5. Tabula libri prescripti (list of homilies) 191
    Kalendarum istius libri 191
    Abhominacio—Signum (imperfect).
    In double columns.

III. 3. 5   C. M. A. 4
238. LACTANTIUS.

Paper, 11⅝ × 8½, ff. 186, double columns of 44 lines. Cent. xv
(1424), in a current hand.   Initials in blue and red.
Collation: 1¹⁰–18¹⁰ 19⁶.

Contents:

1. Extracts about Lactantius, 2 from Augustine and 3 from Jerome f. 1
    Firmiani Lactantii Diuinarum Institutionum libri septem in-
    cipiunt contra gentes .   .   .   . 1 *b*
    Primus liber lactantii de falsa religione.
        Magno et excellenti ingenio viri.
    The Greek quotations are transliterated into the ordinary
    cursive.
    Lib. VII ends f. 153: a domino consequamur.   Expl. liber
    Lact. septimus et ultimus diuinarum Institutionum adu.
    gentes, videl. de vita beata.
    Then a note added rather later: Si cupis hos libros magis
    emendatos habere vade ad Italiam ad Abbaciam nonantule
    Cisterciensis ordinis territorii Bononiensis et dur^d(?)(?ducatus)
    mutinensis et ibi reperies originalem librum ipsius lactancii
    scriptum manu sua.
2. Aug. in lib. vicesimo secundo de civ. dei.   Nullus vel negat
    vel dubitat .   .   .   . 153 *b*
    Inc. liber Lactantii de ira dei.
    Animaduerti sepe Donate
        —et nunquam vereamur iratum.   Expl. lib. Lact. de ira dei.
3. Inc. liber Lactantii de opificio dei .   .   .   .   . 170 *b*
        Quomodo minime sim quietus.
    Ends 186 *b*: ad iter celeste direxerit.   Expl. libri lact. videl.
    septem sui libri Instit. diuin. adu. gentes cum ipsius libris de
    ira dei et opificio dei [et] siue formacione hominis (siue de
    opif. dei *erased*).

Finitum ac scriptum fuit presens opus per manus petri leeuwen
de beka rectoris scolar' sancti saluatoris brugensis a. d. mᵒccccᵒ.
vicesimo quarto in profesto b. v. et martiris Christi katherine.
Unde laudetur deus benedictus cum maria matre sua virgine
gloriosa. Amen.

III. 3. 6   C. M. A. 33

239. Psalter.

Vellum, 11⅛ × 7⅔, ff. 126, 25 lines to a page.   Cent. xv, in a fine
upright narrow English hand, with good ornaments.
Collation : 1⁸–13⁸ 14⁶ | 15⁸ 16⁸.

Contents :

1. Psalterium cum Canticis secundum usum Sarum . . . f.   1
   Antiphons and Responses are given.
   The Cantica begins on f. 95.   The Litany ends f. 107 *b*
       Nunc finem feci da michi quod merui.
   Three blank leaves follow.
   The initials to the Nocturnes (divisions of the Psalter) are of
   very fine English work, usually filled with shaded pink or
   blue foliage.
2. Simplex pertraccio deliciarum uirginis gloriose et quedam
   ipsius deduccio a principio sanctificacionis usque ad apicem
   glorificacionis.   Prelibacio sequencium et excitacio deuocionis   111
       Salue sancta mater dei.   Radix uite robur spei.   Mortis
       in angustiis.
   A series of rhyming salutations ending f. 113.
       hoc nutriri da dulcore. ad optatum glorie. Amen.
   Alia oracio etc.   Stabat mater   113
   Or. ad b. Annam.   Anna salue generosa. de regali stirpe nata   113 *b*
   Rubric : Has uideas laudes qui sacra uirgine gaudes etc. .   114 *b*
       Salue uirgo uirginum (the Salue regina, farced with
       rhyming quatrains).
   O intemerata 117, Obsecro te 118.
   Rubric : quicunque hec septem gaudia etc. . . . .   119 *b*
       Uirgo templum trinitatis.
   Prayers.   Deprecor te sanctissima 120.   *Ad ymaginem*
   d. n. I. C. Omnibus consideratis. Ad S. Joh. Evang. 122 *b*.
   Omnip. sempiterne deus qui unigenitum 122 *b*.   Deus qui
   manus 123.   Angele sancte dei 123.   Anima I. C. 124.
   D. I. C. qui hanc sacratissimam 124.   D. I. C. qui dixisti
   nolo mortem 124 *b*.
   (Pro omnibus temptacionibus) Suppliciter te deus 125.   Concede
   michi queso misericors 125.   Salue sancta facies 126.
   126 *b* is blank.

III. 3. 7   vac.

240. PUPILLA OCULI.

Vellum, 10¾ × 7¾, ff. 151, double columns of 55 lines. Cent. xv early, in a fair hand.

Given in 1667 by Tho. Leigh S.T.B. Below, on f. 1, is: Henricus Goche (xvi) and : praetium 0–5–0.

Collation: 1¹² (wants 1) 2¹²–13¹² (wants 9–12).

Contents:

Table. Abbas—Ypocrisis. Signed "quod R. S."   . . . f.   1
Capitula   9
Text. Humane condicio nature   10
Pars x ends f. 151 *b*: et sic tractatus iste sub numero denerio parcium terminatur.
Expl. tract. qui dicitur pupilla oculi, editus a mag. Johanne de Burgo Cancellario uniuersitatis Cantibrigg' et sacre pagine professore anno domini Ihesu Christi mill^mo ccc^mo lxxxv^to. Deo gracias.
A rebus follows: Two tuns connected by two double-headed darts
⟺ : in the middle R.

III. 3. 8   C. M. A. 14

241. LYRA ETC.

Vellum (and paper), 10⅝ × 7¾, ff. 155, 46 lines to a page. Cent. xv (1474), clearly written.

Collation: 1⁸ (2–7 paper) 2⁸ (2–7 paper) 3¹⁰ 4⁸–14⁸ 15¹⁰–19⁸ (7 stuck to cover: wants 8).

From the Carthusians of Sheen.

Contents :

1. Notabilia et exposiciones secundum eundem (sc. doctorem de lira) super euangelium b. marci .   .   .   .   .   . f.   1
In prologo primo. Sciendum quia plura euangelia et a pluribus.
Notabilia super Lucam 2. Super Gen. iii. 4 *b*. Super Levit. xviii. 7 with other notes.
Hic inc. septem regule xeponendi (!) sacram scripturam quas tangit ysidorus in primo libro de summo bono ca°. xx°. Et uocantur iste regule ab aliquibus claues .   .   .   .   8 *b*
Lyra on Gen. vi. 9 *b*. On Gen. xlix. 10. On Deut. xxxiii. 14.
2. Inc. deuota oracio ven. Bonauenture ad S. trinitatem .   .   17 *b*
In fide summe et indiuidue trinitatis obsecro.

Inc. tabula meditacionum vite Ihesu Christi sec. Bonauenturam f. 18
Inc. prologus meditacionum vite Saluatoris nostri I. C.
dulcissimi 19
Inter alia virtutum et laudum
—et ideo de ipsis videamus.
c. i. Cum per longissima tempora 20
c. cxxi. De modo meditandi etc. ends 86 *b*, subesse desingnauit.
hec Bernardus. Et sic finitur liber. Deo gracias (bis).
Expl. medit. quas composuit ven. Cardinalis Bonauentura, de
vita passione et morte saluatoris nostri I. C. deo gracias.
3. Inc. vita S. Jacobi apostoli vocati fratris domini cum noua
addicione . . . . 86 *b*
Cogitaui ego quidem carthusiensis monachus illo nomine in-
dignus predicator et rudis,
He seems to take the text of the Legenda Aurea and expound it.
Ends f. 103: Osanna in excelsis. Saluum fac in celis, quo
nos perducat qui uiuit et regnat deus per omnia sec. sec.
Amen.
Expl. vita b. Jacobi ap. vocati fratris domini cum noua addicione, quam apposuit quidam monachus modicus et minutus
sed mis*er* magnus in domo Ihesu de bethleem iuxta schene
a.d. 1°4°7°4° tempore messis. Deo gracias. Aspice in me
domine et miserere mei secundum iudicium diligencium
nomen tuum. Amen.
4. Inc. tabula super Bibliam. Genesis i. Creauit deus celum et
terram . . . . 103 *b*
An epitome of each chapter of the Bible.
Ends f. 147. qui apposuerit vel diminuerit de verbis prophecie
libri huius etc.
Expl. tabula super bibliam. Deo gracias.
A table of subjects 107
5. Extracts from the Revelations of St Bridget (?). In another hand 149
Herba (Verba) Christi ad sponsam. Ego adhuc sic caritatiue
diligo animam tuam ut antequam ea carerem adhuc iterum si
possibile esset cruci affigerer.
Ends f. 152: et cum terra de terrenis sustentatur, dominus terre
a terra sua ad iram non prouocetur.

III. 3. 9   C. M. A. 31

242. MISSAL.

Vellum, 10½ × 7¼, ff. 265, double columns of 39 lines. Cent. xi
early, in fine narrow upright English hand, with good borders and
initials.
Given in 1667 by Tho. Leigh.

Collation: 1⁸–33⁸ 34² (2 canc.).

A note by Mr Bradshaw says " most ordinary xvth century."

Contents :

Scribbled at the end
    me selfe dyd wryte yt.
    tu et ego sumus in toto.

The Sanctoral appears to be purely Sarum.

The divisions of the book and the principal feasts have fine full
    borders of pink and blue with white patterns, in very good style.

III. 3. 10

243.

Vellum, cir. 10 × 7, ff. 218 + 1, 37 lines and double columns of 37
and 46 lines.   Cent. xv and xiv, in several hands.

2 fo. xvii de resurreccione
or critudine.

Collation: 1 flyleaf.   1¹²–4¹² 5⁸ 6¹²–10¹² (wants 12) 11⁸ 12⁸ 13¹²–
18¹² | 19¹² (wants 12) | 20⁴.

Contents :

1. Epistola ven. Ysidori Ep. ad beatum Mansorium coepiscopum
    de lapsis (LXXXIII. 898) . . . . f.   1
    Ueniente ad nos famulo uestro…nicetio
    —aut pocior extat auctoritas.
    Followed immediately by the Capitula of the Sententiae of
    Isidore.

2. Sententiae Isidori (LXXXIII. 537) 2
    Summum bonum deus est
        —beatificandos includit. Amen. Amen.
    Expl. lib. tercius b. Ysidori hispaniensis Archiep.

3. Gregorius in suis pastoralibus (LXXVII. 13) .   .   .   . f. 57
   Capitula.
   Prologus aliqualis. Quia melius fuerat.
   Text. Pastoralis cure me pondera fugere
   —manus leuet. Amen. Expl. Greg. in suis pastoralibus.
4. De sex alis confessionis (Alani de Insulis)   100
   Prima ala confessio est
   —finem beatitudine. Amen.
5. Pastorale b. Ambrosii (XVII. 567)   103
   Si quis, fratres, oraculum
   —promisisti perpetua. Amen. Expl. pastorale Ambr.
6. Meditationes b. Bernardi   106
   Multi multa sciunt.
7. Augustinus in libro omeliarum (XL. 1113) .   .   .   .   124 b
   Penitentes penitentes.
8. Meditationes b. Edmundi (Speculum Ecclesiae) .   .   .   126
   In nomine d. n. I. C. Amen. Iste liber est qui docet uiuere
   perfecte etc.
   Uidete ad quod uocati estis
   —ab origine mundi per eum qui etc.
         Expl. Spec. S. Edmundi.
   In a late hand. The Apostles' Creed divided into clauses, each
   assigned to an Apostle.
9. De semptem regulis Ticonjj (XVIII. 15)   138
   Nota versus pro regulis Tyconii quas tractat Aug. 3° de
   doctrina christiana.
   Regula prima caput nostrum cum corpore iungit etc.
   Nota hic bene expositionem decem regularum.
   f. 141 containing the end is only a fragment.
10. Inc. Bonauentura (Meditationes de passione)   .   .   .   142
   Adueniente iam et iminente
   —uiuit et regnat. Amen. Expl. medit. de passione
   christi quas compilauit Bonau. Cardinalis.
11. Inc. themata de epistolis (dominicalibus per annum) .   .   151 b
   Abiciamus opera.
   Themata euangeliorum   153
12. Tabula super bibliam .   .   .   .   155 b
   Abstinencia. precepit deus ade. to Zelus.
13. Continencia et distinccio librorum sacre scripture .   .   .   174
   Requiris a me karissime ut tibi quid in uno quoque libro.
   Uolenti post hec omnia poma [mea] noua et uetera.
   Principium ergo exponendi a genesi sumamus
   —prope est dies etc.
14. Table of Gospels and Epistles for the year   187
15. Augustinus de uisitacione infirmorum (XL. 1147) .   .   .   190
   Visitacionis gracia.
16. Inc. liber Aug. ad petrum diaconem de fide trinitatis (XL. 753)   194 b
   Epistolam fili petre.

17. Inc. tract. de peccato originali editus a fr. Egidio Romano
ord. heremitarum S. Aug. qui iuxta sui nominis literas vii
capit terminum.

Ego cum sim puluis
—te uidere possimus qui es bened. in sec. sec.   Amen.
Expl. tract. de pecc. orig., editus ab Egidio rom. ord. fr. herem.

18. In an earlier hand, in double columns (cent. xiv).
S. Augustini speculum peccatorum (XL. 983)   .   .   . f. 204
Fratres karissimi quam tremenda est dies illa
—nouissima tua prudenter prouideas. Expl. spec. pecc.
Aug. etc. quod fecit in fine uite sue.

19. (Qualiter debet sacerdos interrogare peccatores)   .   .   . 213 b
Uniuersitas peccati sicut dicit b. Iacobus
—insufficienter repellantur.   Expl. iste tract.

20. In another hand.
Epitome of the Bible in verse often attributed to Alexander
Neckham : one word to each chapter   215
(Genesis). Sex. prohibet. peccant. Abel. enoch. archa fit. intrant
...
(Apoc.).   Flebunt. ad cenam. surgunt. sponsam. uenio iam.
There are a good many marginal scribbles of cent. xvi.

III. 3. 11   vac.

244. PALLADIUS.

Vellum, 10⅛ × 6¾, ff. 70, 27 lines to a page. Cent. xii, in an
exquisite round hand.   Initials mostly in red and green.

Collation: 1⁷ (four left) 2⁸ (wants 3) 3⁸ 4⁸ (wants 5) 5⁸ (? wants
1–3, 6) 6⁸ 7⁸ 8⁸ (wants 3–5, 8) 9⁸ (wants 4–6) 10⁸ (wants 2) 11⁸
(wants 2, 6).

Contents :

Fragments of Palladius de re rustica.
About 20 leaves are gone at the beginning. Begins in I. xxxvii, p. 44, ed. Teubner.
Fictilia deterrima sunt que et hieme gelantur.
On f. 3. Tituli mensis Ianuarii.
The text, which has many lacunae, goes down to November. XII. c. viii (vii).
De pomis aliorum mensium
—quas postea possumus inferre (inserere, p. 243, l. 25).

There are some old pencil scribbles, but nothing that I have
seen throwing light on the history of the MS.

It has been very neatly bound and made up at some time in
cent. xviii, with blank paper leaves to show the lacunae.

III. 3. 12   C. M. A. 103

245. Jo. Colet in 1 ad Corinthios.

Vellum, 9⅝ × 6¼, ff. 120 + 2, 22 lines to a page.   Cent. xvi early, in a very fine clear Roman hand, doubtless that of Peter Meghen, Colet's usual scribe.

Ex dono M^{ri} Anthonii Tuckney in Sac. Theol. Baccalaurei et hujus Coll. Socii.

Collation: 1 flyleaf.   1⁸–15⁸ (a–p).   1 flyleaf.

Contents :

> Title in black letter by another hand.
> Commentaria Jo^{is} Coleti sacrae theologiae professoris. decani eccle-
> siae S. pauli London in epistolam diui Pauli ad Corinthios 1ᵃ.
> Paulus quem deus voluit apo (so far in capitals) -stolum Jesu Christi
> esse saluatoris: Corinthios simul et omnes ubique locorum qui
> inuocant dominum Jesum : eis optat graciam et pacem a deo
> patre et domino Jesu.   Gaudet deinde et gratulatur Corinthiis.
> Ends f. 120 *b*:· Marhanatha hebreo uerbo asserit Paulus et affirmat
> dominum uenisse.
> Various blanks are left in the text as if the archetype were illegible.
> It is stated by Mr J. H. Lupton in the preface to his edition of
> these Lectures on 1 Cor. (1874) that this copy is made from what
> is most likely Colet's autograph, namely, the University Library
> MS. Gg. 4. 26.

III. 3. 13   C. M. A. 10

246. Horae in English.

Vellum, 9⅞ × 6½, ff. 67 + 3, 28 lines to a page.   Cent. xiv late, well written and ornamented.

Collation: 1 flyleaf.   1⁶ 2⁸–8⁸ (wants 6) 9⁶, 2 flyleaves.

On f. 31

> John Comber Shermanbury (?) (xv, xvi).

On the flyleaf notes by Farmer and another.

Contents :

  But siþ cloþyng of þis loue is so myche loued of god
  —and wite who wente amys. Here endiþ þe xvi propretees
  of charite. 67 a, 68 b and flyleaves blank.
This Prymer is described by Maskell, *Mon. Rit.* II. xxxiv.
In the Kalendar David and Chad do not occur. At May 21 in red
  is an original entry. Here was þe erþe quake þe ȝeer of oure
  lord m. ccc. lxxxij. June 28 Seynt lyoun.
At July 16, in black. King Richard was crowned þe ȝeer of oure
  lord m. ccc. lxxvij°.
Sept. 2. Seynt antelyn.
Thomas of Canterbury erased in December: but his translation in
  July not touched.
Each of the hours has a fine initial and partial border of good bold
  English work, with a good deal of gold.
This MS. is not specially noticed (so far as I can see) in the E. E. T. S.
  edition of the *Lay Folk's Mass-book* by Mr Littlehales.

III. 3. 14

247. De naturis rerum.   C. M. A. 112

Vellum, $9\frac{3}{4} \times 6\frac{1}{2}$, ff. 89 + 1, double columns of 35 lines. Cent. xv, clearly written.

Collation: 1 flyleaf. 1^8–10^8 (wants 2, 3) 11^{10} 12 (one left).

On f. 1

God send vs heauen after thys lyfe And that shall we have if we liue accordinglye M (monogram) W. (xvi).

Contents :

Compilatio de naturis rerum.
Compilacio de libris naturalibus Aristotelis et aliorum quorundam
  philosophorum de rerum natura. Que quidem compilacio quinque in se continet partes principales, Quarum prima principalis

in octo subdiui(di)tur partibus prima que agit de primo principio
s. de deo subsequencia habet capitula.
De unitate et simplicitate dei etc.
Capitula end f. 6 *a*.
Prologue. Cum omne desiderii compos et maxime creatura rationa-
bilis appetat suam perfectionem . . . . . . f. 6 *b*
—a digniori inchoandum est ab ipso sumamus exordium secundum
hec capitula.
c. 1. Dicit Aristoteles in x ph*ilosophie* p^ie Deus inquid est unus
eternus nobilis.
The contents of the other parts are
I. 2. de creaturis. 3. de corporibus animatis. 4. de natura
animalium. 5. de homine. 6. de motu et tempore et loco.
7. de rebus rationalibus. 8. de rebus moralibus.
II. dicitur liber ethicorum Aristotelis.
III. vetus ethice Aristotelis (de fortitudine).
IV. noua ethica Aristotelis (de summo bono).
V. de diffinicionibus rerum et ethimologiis.
Aristotle, Tullius in Rethorica, Boethius de disciplina scolarum
and others are quoted.
Ends f. 89: adnichilantur per infusionem aque calide inter uulnera
etc. belche c^i.
Expl. libellus de secretis nature.

III. 3. 15. Printed Book.

III. 3. 16   C. M. A. 121

248. OFFICIA ECCLESIASTICA.

Vellum, 10 × 7½, ff. 48, double columns of 30 lines. Cent. xv,
clearly written in a rather ugly hand.
Given by Th. Leigh, S.T.B. in 1667.
Collation: 1⁸–5⁸ | gap | 6⁸.
Scribbles at the end:

dum sumus in mundo uiuamus corde iocundo etc.

Contents:

Office for the feast of Corpus Christi . . . . . . f. 1
In festo Corporis Christi ad uesperas. Antiphona.
Sacerdos in eternum.
On the lower margin of f. 2 (xv, xvi)
Quillermus hennyson filius Quillermi Hennison qui fuit filius
Johannis Gray. amen amen.

III. 3. 17
249.

Paper, 9¾ × 7, ff. 16.   Cent. xvii–xviii, well written.

Εὐνομίου τοῦ δυσσεβοῦς ἀπολογητικὸς πρὸς ὃν ἔγραψε τοὺς ἀντιρρη-
τικοὺς ὁ μέγας Βασίλειος (Migne, *P. G.* XXX. 835).

Τὸ μὲν (οὖν) συκοφαντεῖν καὶ διαβάλλειν
  —καὶ δυνάμει τοῦ υἱοῦ γενόμενον.

Τέλος τοῦ Εὐνομίου.

Collated in part with a printed edition. Archbishop Tenison had a manuscript of the work, which was used by Cave (*Hist. Lit.* I. 220).

III. 3. 18   C. M. A. 106
250. STATII THEBAIS.

Vellum, 9⅝ × 5⅔, ff. 85, 52 lines to a page.   Cent. xiii early, in two beautiful regular hands.   2 fo. Turba minor.

At the end (xvi–xvii)

IOHN STOCKE I [a device] S.

On f. 1 at top (xiv)

Stacius ad Thebaid.

Collation: 1⁸–5⁸ (wants 2, 3, 5) 6⁸–8⁸ 9¹⁰ (7, 8 canc.) 10⁸ 11¹⁰ (wants 9, 10 blank).

P. Papinii Statii Thebaidos libri XII.

F(raternas acies: *added later*) alternaque regna prophanis. Handsome initial with gold and silver.

Lib. II. f. 8. III. f. 15. IV. f. 22. V. f. 30.

After V. 470 f. 34, reuoluitur annus is a lacuna of 208 lines (the contents of *two* leaves) up to 679 (Amphioraus ait), but only *one* leaf has been cut out. However, *two* leaves have been cut out *before* f. 34. There may have been a bad displacement which led to the 3 leaves being cut out and lost.

VI. f. 35 *b*. After VI. 224 (f. 37) cingula flammis is a lacuna to VII. 118, Erigit attoniti. Here (at f. 38) the hand changes up to 44 *a* in which the 1st hand resumes.

VIII. f. 44 *b*. IX. f. 52. There is perhaps a change of hand at f. 57, more certainly at f. 62. X. f. 61. XI. f. 70. XII. f. 77. Ends f. 85 *a*. referentur honores.

The earlier books II, III, IV, V, have arguments in verse. VI. has one line only. VII. is defective. VIII. has longer verse argument.

IX–XII. have no arguments.

On f. 85 *b* is a grammatical note in pencil of cent. xiv.

The MS. is mentioned by Bentley on Hor. *Ep.* I. 6. 59. It has recently been examined by Dr Postgate.

III. 3. 19   C. M. A. 13

251. HIPPIATRICA.

Vellum and paper, 9⅝ × 6½, ff. 187, 22 and 24 lines to a page. Cent. xii and xiv. There is no donor's name. In the cover is pasted an old label (xvii, xviii)

Βιβλίον Ἱππιατρικὸν. Liber magni pretii quoad partem primam scriptus accuratius. plurima continet quae in libro typis excuso (scil. Basileae 1537) non comparent.

Collation: 1⁸ (wants 1) 2⁸ 3⁷ (see below) 4⁸ (see below) 5 (see below) 6⁸ 7⁸ 8⁸ 9⁷⁸ (wants 4, 5) 10⁸ 11¹² 12⁸ 13⁸ 14⁸ (wants 4, 5) 15⁸ ‖ 16⁸–22⁸ ‖ 23⁸ 24¹⁰.

Quire 3 has six leaves apparently continuous: then a gap: then a pair of leaves on the second of which is the signature γ′.

After quire 4 (p. 38) a gap is marked.

Of quire 5 only two leaves remain: a gap is marked after the first.

After quire 8 a gap is marked.

Quire 9 has perhaps lost the middle sheet.

There are old signatures in black at the ends of the quires, and original signatures in red at the beginning of quires 13–15, quires 16–23 are numbered a'–n'. The pagination is of cent. xvii? The leaves have been mended with bits of more than one Latin MS. seemingly of cent. xii.

A transcript now in the Gale collection at Trinity College (O. 9. 16) was made from this MS. in 1673. P. Needham used the original to some extent in his edition of the *Geoponica*, Cambridge, 1704. Accounts of it were given by Daremberg, *Notices et extraits des Manuscrits médicaux* (Paris, 1853, p. 169 sqq.) who used largely notes made by Bussemaker.

A fuller account by Eugen Oder is in *Rheinisches Museum* LI. (1896), pp. 52–80. He had the use of the MS. at Berlin during the summer of 1891.

A full edition of the text may be expected in the near future. I shall therefore not attempt to give a complete list of the chapters, but only to point out the external peculiarities and arrangement of the MS.

It begins with an incomplete table of contents.

μς´ (in red) περὶ ἐρπιστοῦ καὶ ἐπινυκτίδος . . . . . f.   1 a
and ending f. 2 a ρθ´ (in red) περὶ σκευασίας ἐγχυματισμῶν.
f. 2 b is covered with carefully washed out writing: cursive, of nearly the same date as the MS. itself.
f. 3 (p. 1) begins with a rubric.
περὶ ἀρετῆς ἵππου πρόγνωσις ἐκ προσώπου   1
Ἡ τοῦ ἵππου ἀρετή, ἐκ πρώτης ὑποφαίνεται τῆς ἡλικίας.
The other rubrics are:
ἵππου ὀχέτου ἔκλεξις καὶ χρόνος τῆς ὀχείας   1
κυουσῶν ἵππων ἐπιμέλεια   4
πώλων ἀπὸ γέννης ἐπιμέλεια   4
πότε δαμασθῆναι δεῖ τοὺς ἵππους καὶ πῶς   6
ἵππου ἀγαθοῦ δοκιμασία   6
ἵππου σκολιοῦ δοκιμασία   8
ἵππων φύσεις κατὰ ἔθνος   8
Ἀρμένιοι ἵπποι κατὰ σῶμα μὲν εὐμεγέθεις.
Alphabetical, ending with Λυρκανοὶ ("Υρκανοι)
—κάλλιστοι παιδοτρόφοι.
ἀρχὴ τοῦ ἱπποιατρικοῦ βιβλίου τοῦ οὕτω καλουμένου, ἡ μέλισσα .   11
πυρέσσων ἵππος ἔχει τὴν κεφαλὴν καταρρέπουσαν . . .   12

There are a good many interlinear and marginal glosses in very black ink, in a much contracted hand, which I suppose to be of the xvth century. They continue to the end of the volume.

Obvious lacunae occur after pp. 38, 58, 60, 222, in chapters 3–4 (= 2, 3 printed ed.), 7–8 (= 9–11), 56–57 (= 68, 69).

The volume is partially palimpsest: see especially pp. 143, 145, 149, 156, 158, 165, 167, 169, 172–4, 187, 190, 198, 203, 209, 211, 213, 216, 218, 220. The older writing is in Greek uncials of cent. viii (?) consisting of a comment in sloping uncials on a text in upright uncials. Hardly enough has been deciphered to pronounce with certainty what the treatise is: but it is clearly Christian, and perhaps a commentary on the Pauline Epistles, apparently not by Chrysostom.

The first hand ceases at f. 222 in the chapter (56) περὶ ἰσχναινομένων ἵππων (=c. 68 of the edition of 1537). The section with which it ends does not seem to be in the printed editions.

The second hand, which is a very pretty round one, continues on p. 223 in c. 57 (περὶ ψώρας)=59 of the printed edition.

θεομνήστου εἰσ τὸ αὐτὸ. ἡ ψώρα ἐν τοῖς ἵπποις (p. 190, ed. 1537). I cannot tell whether more than one leaf is wanting: two would be the most, I think.

The paper leaves begin at p. 334 (really 335) in c. 92 (περὶ εἴδους ἐπιλογῆς ἵππων = c. 144, ed. 1537).

They end p. 369 (370) in c. 109 περὶ σκευασίας ἐγχυματισμῶν=c. 128, ed. 1537. The last paragraph beginning: Ἴρεως ἰλλυρικῆς· ἀριστολόγχης μακρᾶς γεντιάνης, does not seem to be in the printed text.

The last thing on the last page is a fragmentary rubric

σκ(ευασία) .. πικοα...

The writing on the vellum leaves (after p. 222) and on the paper seems to me to be the same. It can hardly be earlier than cent. xiii.

III. 3. 20   Printed Book.

III. 3. 21

252.   EUSEBIUS DE MORTE HIERONYMI.
KALENDARIUM.

Vellum, 10½ × 7½, ff. 48 + 12, two volumes.   Cent. xiv and xii late. Vol. II given by Joshua Barnes.

I. *Collation:* 1⁸–6⁸, 28 lines to a page, good French hand, rather current.

At the end an erased inscription (following the colophon)

Iste liber est magistri petri blanchuilli magistri ...perl...

Contents :

Inc. epistola b. eusebii ad sanctum damasium pontinensem episcopum et ad christianissimum theodonium Romanorum senatorem
de morte gloriosissimi confessoris Jeronimi doctoris magnifici.
Patri Reuerendissimo Damasio pontiniensi episcopo et christia-
nissimo Theodonio Romanorum senatori Eusebius olim ieronimi
sanctissimi discipulus.
Ends f. 47 b : in futuro gaudia que iam tu possides adipisci. Beati
Eusebii ad S. Dam. pont. ep. et ad theod. rom. Senat. de morte
glor. conf. Jeron. doctoris magnif. epistola expl. feliciter.
On f. 1 is a very good miniature and partial border of ivy-leaf work,
and initial. The picture represents the death of St Jerome. The
ground a chequer of lozenges blue, red and gold. In a house
with blue roof, door on left, Jerome lies (head to *R*.) in bed with
red and gold quilt. He is nimbed and bearded. Two demi-
angels in air receive his soul (a nude figure proceeding from his
mouth). At the head of the bed a wooden chair. At the foot a
stone seat on which Eusebius in blue sits writing on a scroll on
his knee. He is bearded, not nimbed.
f. 48 blank.

II. *Collation :* a¹⁰ (wants 2, 8), b⁴. Cent. xii late, in a fine
English hand.

The preliminary leaves of what must have been a very fine
Psalter.

1. Table of Concurrentes for the Paschal cycle of 19 years . f. 1
   Also a late scrap of music and a scribble. Suscipe uerbum uirgo.
   f. 1 b ruled into squares but blank.
2. (Calendar) wanting December, in red, blue and black, with
   gold initials 2
   Jan. 7. Obitus Rogeri prioris IX added in black.
   Feb. 13. Eormenilde V.
       23. Mildburge V.
   Mar. 1. Dauid C.
       2. Cedde Ep. in red.
       19. Joseph sponsi S. Marie.
       26. Dominus in sepulcro in red.
   Ap. 11. Guthlaci C.
       19. Alphegi Ep. M. in red.
       29. Transl. S. Ædmundi Reg. M.
       30. Ærkenwaldi Ep. in blue with octave.
   May 26. Augustini Ep. et Bede presb. in blue.
   June 1. Simeonis C.
       3. Erasmi M. added late.
       4. Ob. Beatricis Tyrill.
       14. Ædburge V.
       16. Botulfi Abb.

	23.	Ætheldrithe V.
	30.	Ob. pie memorie dom. Joh. Bradwell prioris.
July	2.	Dep. S. Swithuni in red. Visitation added.
	6.	Sexburge.
	7.	Hedde Ep.
	8.	Grimbaldi C.
	11.	Transl. S. Benedicti in blue with octave.
	13.	Mildrithe V. in blue.
	15.	Transl. S. Swithuni Ep. in blue.
Aug.	2.	Aethelwoldi in red.
	5.	Osuualde R. M. in red.
Sept.	3.	Ordinacio S. Gregorii in red.
	22.	Maurici cum soc. in blue.
	24.	Conceptio S. Joh. Bapt.
	27.	Cosme et Damiani in red.
Oct.	1.	Remigi Germani Vedasti.
	3.	Duorum euualdorum.
	6.	Fidis in red.
	10.	Paulini Ep.
	11.	Ætfrom Æthelburge V. in red.
	12.	Wilfridi.
	16.	Sancti gereone, duplex festum, added late.
	18.	Ætheldrithe V. in red.
	23.	Romani Ep. in red.
	24.	Festiuitas sanctarum reliquiarum in blue.

The obit of John Bradwell, prior, on Ap. 30 shows that the Psalter once belonged to the Augustinian Priory of Holy Trinity, Aldgate, London, of which Bradwell was Prior in 1513. The prominence given to SS. Erkenwald and Ethelburga would without this have induced me to call the kalendar a London one.

A series of pictures, two on a page, in frames worked with green. The backgrounds are plain, and there is hardly any gold; the principal colours are red and green: the latter has corroded the vellum in some cases. The designs are good: the execution also good, but not of the first class.

1. Annunciation. Angel on *L.*, scroll *Aue—tecum* (inscription later). Virgin stands at desk, *R.* portion of background coloured dark blue.

2. Visitation. The two personages embrace.

3. Nativity. Virgin in bed, head to *L.* Curtain above her. Manger with Child, and heads of ox and ass in air. Joseph seated on *R.* with staff.

4. Angel and Shepherds. Angel stands on *L.* with palm. Three Shepherds. Below, sheep, goat and cow.

5. The Magi journeying. Three kings on horseback with crowns and sceptres, one points *R.*, one *L.*, one full-face.

6. Magi and Herod. Herod seated in *C*. with *L*. leg drawn up on to his throne:
facing him a page sits on the ground supporting a sword hilt upwards. The three kings
stand on *R*.

7. Adoration of the Magi. The Virgin crowned, and Child, seated on *L*. She
holds up an orb with plant springing from it. The three kings hold up vessels.

8. Magi warned. The three kings in bed, one listens to small angel in air with scroll.

9. Flight. Joseph leads the ass to *L*., youth follows.

10. Massacre of Innocents. Two soldiers in mail, with helmets which have nose-
pieces. Each kills a child held by its mother, one with sword, the other with spear.
Herod seated on *R*., a small imp on his neck.

11. Presentation. Joseph on *L*. with basket of doves. The Virgin holds up the
Child. Symeon behind an altar on *R*.

12. Baptism. John on *L*. Christ in heaped-up water. Angel on *R*. holds tunic.
The outer portion of the next leaf is torn off.

13. Feast of Cana. Behind a table Christ, the Virgin, the Governor of the Feast.
In front, the jars and a servant.

14. Raising of Lazarus. Christ stands at the feet of Lazarus, a brown body lying
in marble coffin. Behind it Mary and another (Martha) holding her nose.

15. Temptation (1). The Devil horned with winged shoulders and feet. Christ
seated on a mount on *R*. with scroll. Vade Satana non tentabis dominum.

16. Temptation (2). A towered building. Christ on the roof on *R*. The devil, a
squat figure with stick-like legs in air on *L*. Gold vessels in air by him. Fragment of
another devil falling headlong on *L*.

17. Entry into Jerusalem. Gate on *L*., six heads (and figures) in openings above:
some throw down leaves. In front three, one with palm, two stripping themselves.
Christ rides to *L*. (colt, very small, follows): on *R*., Peter with key and four other Apostles.

18. Washing of Feet. Christ on *L*. touching the feet of Peter, who touches his head.
Other Apostles seated in a group, some drying their feet.

19. Last Supper. Behind a table Christ and John in His bosom in *C*. On *L*. a
group of Apostles with Peter. On *R*. another group. Two Apostles have cups. In
front Judas kneels, receives the sop and takes a fish from the dish.

20. Betrayal. Christ and Judas in *C*. Peter on *L*. pulls back Malchus' head by
the hair. Assailants (one with lantern) on *L*. and *R*.

A blank page. Then the full-page B. initial to Ps. i. Beatus vir, which has lost
nearly all its colour (originally very rich) by rubbing. The body of the letter has a fine
tree with nine figures and half-figures in the branches (3 in *C*.). At the angles are
four medallions. Those on *L*. and *R*. at top are single figures. At bottom on *L*. is
David slinging at Goliath, on *R*. cutting off his head. There has been a good deal of
gold on this leaf.

III. 3. 22   C. M. A. 32

253. PSALTERIUM GRAECE.

Vellum, 10⅝ × 7¼, ff. 26 + 1, 24 lines to a page. Cent. xii, in
two very peculiar large hands, which are doubtless an unskilled
imitation of a Greek cursive hand.

Collation: 1⁸ (marked xi on 8th leaf) 2⁸ (marked xii) 3 a single sheet of two leaves 4⁸ (marked xxi). There is besides a single leaf, detached, which belongs to quire 3.

Contents :

A fragment of a Greek Psalter consisting of the following portions.
Quire 1 (xi) begins at Ps. lxxi. 14. λιτωρσετε ταs ψυχαs αὐτῶν.
Quire 2 (xii) is continuous with it and goes down to lxxxi. 7. υἱοὶ ὑψίστου πάντες ὑμεῖs δὲ ὡs.
Here a late note (xvii). *Desunt multae paginae.*
In quire 3 f. 17 contains cxxvii. 3. υἱοισί (sic) σου ὡς νεοφυτα ἐλεώ to cxxix. 6. ἀπὸ φυλακῆs πρωίαs μέ(χρι).
The detached leaf contains cxxxi. 11. ωμοσεν κ̄s τω Δαδ̄ to cxxxii. 2. εν τῆs νυξὶν ἐπαρατε τὰs. A note. *Desunt nonnulla.*
f. 18 (last remaining leaf of 3) contains cxxxv. 11. κὲ εξαγαγῶντι τὸν ἰηλ. to cxxxvi. 1. 'Επι τῶν ποταμῶν Βαβι(λωνοs). A note. *Deest pagina.*
Quire 4 (xxi) contains cxxxvii. 4. οτι ἠκουσαν πάντα τὰ ῥιματα. to cxliv. *fin.* κὲ εἰς τὸν ἐῶνα τοῦ ἐῶνοs.

The detached leaf, which should follow f. 17, was restored to the College in April 1895 (through the agency of Mr F. Jenkinson, University Librarian) by the late George Washington Moon, who had purchased it with other fragments. A title of cent. xvii which has been scribbled on it shows that it must have been separated from the volume for over two hundred years.

The remaining complete sheet of quire 3 must have been the second in order i.e. consisting of the 2nd and 7th leaves out of the 8.

The titles, numbers and initials are in red. The letters rest on lines ruled with a dry point.

This MS. has enjoyed a certain celebrity. A facsimile of a few lines is in Astle's *Progress of the art of writing* (pl. 6): in the text (p. 75) he assigns it to cent. x. It is no. 294 in Holmes and Parsons' Septuagint. Lagarde calls it Codex P of the Psalms in his *Genesis graece* and in *Specimen* etc. N⁽ᴰ⁸⁾.

Facsimiles of two pages are given in *Camb. Ant. Soc. Proc.*, Vol. VIII. (1892–3), p. 168 ff. in a paper by the present writer, from which the following paragraphs may be reproduced here.

The interest of the book, briefly stated, lies in this : that it is at least as old as the twelfth century; that it was certainly not written by a Greek (or in Greece); and that it was probably written in England. Several points lead me to the belief in its non-Greek origin : first, the vellum, which is to my mind just like the vellum of Western MSS. and not like that of Greek MSS.; next, the writing, of which more anon; thirdly, certain glosses which I find in it; and fourthly, the signatures of the quires.

The writing is a principal point, naturally. The two pages, facsimiles of which accompany this paper (figs. 1, 2), amply suffice to show the remarkable aspect and character of the MS. They are taken from the two ends of the book ; for, as has been already remarked, the writing, after f. 17, becomes larger and coarser than in the earlier leaves. The impression which one gathers at the first glance is that the scribe has been influenced by Russian or Slavonic writing; but a closer examination shows that what he has been doing is to copy painfully and exactly, letter by letter, from a manuscript written in early minuscules. The slow and laborious character of the work becomes more and more apparent as we look further into the MS.: and the conviction speedily arises that no Greek could possibly have written such a hand as this.

It will not be necessary to go into details about the script. I will, however, just specify that certain *compendia scripturae* occur in the MS. : namely, the ordinary contractions of these words and letters : καὶ, δὲ, αρ, ει, ευ, ος, ου, σσ, υν, ψα, ψι. All of these are formed with the elaborate and painful care that characterizes the rest of the writing.

Next let us speak of the glosses and signatures. Three signatures survive ; xi, xii, xxi : and they are all in Roman figures which I attribute to the twelfth century, and in ink not distinguishable from that of the text. I conclude that they are original, and I ask if, in that case, their occurrence is compatible with the supposition of a Greek origin for the MS.

As for the glosses ; there are only a few of them, but they are in two hands, one of the twelfth, the other of the fifteenth century. The first hand is not much later than the text; it has added a few explanations of words and contractions.

·i· *glutinare*
lxxii. 28.   προσκολλασθε

       legis   *altare*

lxxiii. 1. νομης (a wrong explanation). αγιαστιριον

          erisiue

lxxvii. 46. ερυσιβη

          adipe frumenti

cxlvii. 3. στεατος πυρου

also χειρ *manus,* νωτον *dorsum.*

The contractions explained are :

$$\overline{\pi\rho\omega\nu} \; pateron \quad \overline{\upsilon\upsilon} \; filium.$$

The second hand, writing late in the fifteenth century, has added the opening words of the Psalms in Latin: (e.g. lxxii. *Quam bonus*), and a few explanations of words.

Now it seems to me that both of these hands are English ; about the second hand in particular I feel little doubt.

This second annotator may quite possibly have been the Franciscan Richard Brinkley[1], who at one time owned the Greek Psalter now at Gonville and Caius College, and also the famous Codex Leicestrensis of the New Testament. He was a student of Hebrew as well as of Greek ; for a Hebrew Psalter which belonged to Bury Abbey was lent to him by that house in the year 1502. It is now in the Bodleian Library (Laud. Orient. 174), and contains Latin annotations of a character very similar to those in the Emmanuel Psalter.

According to my theory, then, this Psalter was written in an English monastery in the twelfth century, and was studied as late as the fifteenth century.

III. 3. 23

254. PEERAGE.

Paper, 9⅝ × 6⅞, ff. circ. 80. Cent. xvi, well written.
On the flyleaf :

      Homo cum sis id fac semper intelligas. Thomas Holbech.

---

[1] For an account of Brinkley see Rendel Harris, *The Leicester Codex*, 17 sqq., where, however, the Hebrew Psalter is not mentioned.

Contents:

A chronological Peerage of England, arranged under the reigns of
the Sovereigns from William I to Elizabeth. The shields of the
Sovereigns are left blank.
In the margin are shields neatly tricked in pen and ink.
The text begins
   Edgar Ethelinge sonne too Edward yᵉ outlawe.
A short blazon of the arms is given at the end. The last item is
(post Annum 14 Elizabethae).
ffrederik L. Wynsore g. vn saultier arg. enter 12 croscroslettes or.

III. 3. 24   C. M. A. 107?

255. COMMENT. IN NATURALIA ARISTOTELIS.

Paper, 9 × 7⅜, ff. circ. 200, 39 lines to a page. Cent. xvii, very
neatly written.

Contents:

In uniuersam Aristotelis naturalem philosophiam Commentarii.
   Praeludiis hic nihil opus, consuli enim possunt prolegomena
   Logica.
After the Comment. on the *De anima* follow
   Exercitationes naturales.
      Unde in animo nascantur scientiae. Exercitatio prima.
Extending to the end of the volume.

III. 3. 25   C. M. A. 107?

256. COMMENT. IN NATURALIA ARISTOTELIS.

Paper, 10 × 7, pp. 498, numbered. Cent. xviii (1653), well
written.

Contents:

   Commentarius D. Isaaci Hugonis in physicam Aristotelis.
      Exceptus a me Dauide Primerozio.
      Salmurii Anno 1653.
      The Comment. on the Physica is dated at the end 16 Junii 1653.
2.   Comm. in Libb. de Coelo (27 Junii 1653) .   .   .   . f. 233
3.   ,,   in Libb. de ortu et Intentu (11 Jul. 1653) . . 301
4.   ,,   in Libb. de Anima .   .   .   .   ·   .   . 365

Finis commentariorum in physicam Aristotelis dictatorum a D.
Isaaco Hugone philosophiae professore doctissimo.
A me Dauide Primerozio diligenter exceptorum et absolutorum
28 Jul. 1653.
Followed by a printed sheet (folded) of Theses propounded in
1650 at Saumur by the following Candidates in philosophy.

Isaacus Barberis.	Picto Ruparduensis.
David Primerosius.	Rotomagensis.
Steph. Pallardius.	Picto Niortensis.
Claud. Fautrartius.	Armoricus.
Sam. Portevinus.	Salmuriensis.

III. 3. 26–31. Printed Books.

III. 3. 32

257.

Paper, 9⅛ × 7⅛, ff. 18, interleaved. Cent. xviii, written with extreme neatness and care, in red and black ink.

Purchased in 1895. Formerly in the collection of Sir Thomas Phillipps, no. 3836. It was Lot 121 in the sale at Sotheby's. Craven Ord owned it at one time.

Catalogus Librorum MSS. qui asservantur in Bibliotheca Collegii Emmanuelis apud Cantabrigienses.

There are 116 volumes enumerated, and 14 oriental as against 137 items in the Catalogi MSS. Angliae of 1697: while in this MS. Sancroft's gifts are included, which are not in the other.

There is a very long account of the MS. now numbered I. 3. 6.

III. 3. 33

258.

Paper, 8⅞ × 6½, pp. 67 written, the rest blank. Cent. xviii (1772). Belonged to Cha. Chadwick of Emmanuel (Nov. 4, 1772).

Praelectiones Dialecticae.

By R. Farmer, B.D., Fellow of Em. Coll. Cantab. 1772. Wholly in Latin.

III. 3. 34

259.

Vellum, 6½ × 4⅝, ff. 4, 32 lines to a page.   Cent. xiii late.
Four leaves of a copy of the Satires of Persius, extracted from a binding and inlaid in quarto paper by Dr Shuckburgh, Librarian.
The portions of text comprised in these leaves are:

f. 1, 2.	Sat. III. 57.	Surgentem dextro	to v. 16.	Doctus et.
f. 3.	„ v. 19.	Nec (!) equidem	to 83.	An quisquam.
f. 4 a.	„ v. 157.	Nec tu cum	to 188.	Predictum.
f. 4 b.	„ VI. 1.	Admouit	to 30.	Ingentes.

There are marginal and interlinear glosses.

IV. 1. 17, 18 ⎫
IV. 2. 29   ⎬   C. M. A. 99, 100, 101

260–262.   LETTERS OF THE MARTYRS.

Recently bound in three volumes.   IV. 1. 17 measures 13⅝ × 9¾:
IV. 1. 18, 12½ × 8½: IV. 2. 29, 8½ × 6¼.

260.

IV. 1. 17 has a vellum leaf at each end from a theological MS. in Latin of cent. xv, in double columns.
It contains:

1. Epistle of John Bradford to Richard Hopkyns, 1554.
   8 ff. Parker Society. *Writings of Bradford.* I. 389.
2. f. 9. The same to John Halle, 1555. 2 ff. P. S. II. 216.
3. f. 11. The same. Farewell to Cambridge, 1555. II. 441.
   Although I lok.
4. f. 15. Cranmer to the Lords of the Council. 1 f.
5. f. 16. Bradford. Admonition. I. 407. 2 f.
6. f. 18. Bradford to Hall and wife. II. 216.
*7. f. 20. Rauffe, Allerton to the town of Much Bentley. 5 ff.
   Imperfect. See Foxe VIII. 405.
8. f. 25. Bradford. 2 ff. To Sir James Hales II. 85.
   The God of mercye and father of all comfort.
*9. f. 27. Will Tyms. 1 f. (See Foxe VIII. 107.)

10. f. 28. H. B. (Bullinger) to Hooper. Zurich 1554. 2 ff.
11. f. 30. Bradford to Walden. 2 ff. P. S. I. 455.
12. f. 32. T. Whittle to John Careless. 1 f. Foxe VII. 728.
13. f. 34. J. B(radford) to a faithful woman. 4 ff. (Joyce Hales. P. S. II. 108.
14. f. 38. Robert Samuel to the Christian Congregation. 2 ff. and slips.
Foxe VII. 378.
15. f. 40. Bradford. 2 ff. to Royden. II. 124.
16. f. 42. Laurence Saunders to Mrs Harrington. 2 ff.
*17. f. 44. Lady Vane to Philpot. 1 f.
18. f. 45. Bradford to Mrs Wilkinson etc. The sayme peace that oure sauyour.
2 ff. P. S. II. 45.
19. f. 47. Jo. Simson to congregation in Suffolk etc. 2 ff.
20. f. 49. Anne Knyvett. 2 ff. Cf. Foxe VIII. 553.
21. f. 51. ? to Rob. Glover (Coventry). 1 f. Imperf. See Foxe VII. 384.
22. f. 52. Without heading, unfinished. 2 ff. The grace of allmightie shall
fill you.
23. f. 54. End of a letter of Bradford. 1 f.
24. f. 55. Jo. Simson to the congregation in Suffolk etc. 2 ff. = no. 19.
25. f. 57. Th. Hawkes, general letter. 1 f. 1554.
26. f. 59. = no. 18 (Will. Tymmys at end). 4 ff.
27. f. 63. Bartlets Grene 1556. 2 ff. Foxe VII. 743.
28. f. 65. Philpot to Mrs Harrington. 1 f.
29. f. 66. = no. 18. 2 ff.
30. f. 68. To Tymms. 2 ff. The same ffayth.
31. f. 70. Anonymous. 2 ff.
32. f. 72. Rychard Gybson. 1 f.
33. f. 73. Bradford to a sister. 2 ff.
34. f. 75. Jo. Tuesyn to his wife (?). 2 ff.
35. f. 77. The light off the gospell.
36. f. 79. Bradford to Joyce Hales (?) on her father's death. 3 ff. II. 108.
37. f. 82. Philpot to Careless. The grace off God.
38. f. 83. ? = no. 18. 2 ff.
39. f. 85. Anon. 1 f.
40. f. 86. Anon. On the back Will. Aylesbury. 1 f.
41. f. 87. To Rych. Nycoll etc. prisoners in Newgate. 1 f. folded.
42. f. 88. Anon. 2 ff.
43. f. 90. Imperfect. 1 f.
44. f. 91. Matheus Greston to a prisoner at Bp Stokesleys about 1527. 2 ff.
45. f. 92. John Hallidaie. 2 ff. Imperfect.
46. f. 94. Anon. 2 ff.
47. f. 96. Narrative of Crucifix at Cockram.
48. f. 98. 10 ff. The first 4 leaves follow the last. Bp Ridley's farewell letter.
P. S., p. 395.
49. f. 109. Ridley to the brethren. 2 ff. P. S., p. 349 = no. 145.
50. f. 111. Ridley, ad fratres qui christum cum cruce complectuntur. Latin,
p. 352.
51. f. 112. 1 f. Ridley to Cheke 1551. 2 ff., p. 331.
52. f. 114. Erkenwold Rawlins to Will. Punt (?). 1 f.

53. f. 114*. Ridley to Grindall. 2 ff., p. 388.
54. f. 116. Ridley to Bradford. 1 f. Holograph. P. S. (Bradford) II. 161.
55. f. 117. Ridley to Bradford. Latin Hologr. II. 220.
　　f. 118. Ridley to Bradford. Latin Hologr. II. 206.
56. f. 120. Rawlins to Bradford. II. 97.
57. f. 121. Meditations. 2 ff. Bradford. I. 233.
58. f. 123. Laur. Saunders. Touchynge the cause of myne imprisonment. 1 f.
59. f. 124. Bradford to his mother. II. 41.
60. f. 126. Anon. 1 f. folded. The allmightie God with his most graciouse spirit.
61. f. 128. Jo. Symson=no. 19? 2 ff.
62. f. 130. Jo. Careles. Foxe VIII. 176. 2 ff.
63. f. 130. Jo. Careles to Margery C. 1 f. and flyleaf.
64. f. 134. Jo. Bradford to Eaton. II. 188. Holograph.
65. f. 136. J. Bradford to Mrs Coke. II. 100. Original.
66. f. 138. Bradford, Philpot etc. to Cranmer, Ridley and Latimer, prisoners at
Oxford. P. S. II. 169.
67. f. 139. Anon. Grace marcye and peace.
68. f. 141. Bartlet Grene. I have often herd one argument.
69. f. 142. Leaf of Latin notes on Et adipe frumenti satiat etc.
70. f. 143. Dr Taylor's Will (copy).
71. f. 144. Bradford to a Free-Willer. II. 128.
72. f. 146. Th. Whittle. Fox VII. 725.
73. f. 148. Philpot to John Careles. (VII. 691.)
　　　　　　My dearely beloved brother Careles I have receved.
74. f. 149. Whittle to Filles and Cutbert. (VII. 729.)
75. f. 150. Philpot to the brethren. (VII. 696?)
76. f. 153. J. Hullier. Moste deare Christianes I thynk it verie necessarie.
77. f. 157. The same. (VII. 131.)
78. f. 160. Philpot to a lady. VII. 701.
79. f. 162. To his sister. VII. 694.
80. f. 164. The same. God off all consolation.
81. f. 166. Careles to Bradford. VIII. 174.
82. f. 167. Anon. It reioisith me not a lytle whan I consider.
83. f. 169. Bradford to Shalcross of Lancaster. II. 232.
　　　　　　The peace of conscience in Christ.
84. f. 171*. Woodman to Philpot.
85. f. 172. Philpot. Remember dear sister yᵗ yoʳ liffe.
86. f. 173.=no. 77.
87. f. 175. Anon. I wish to you my good brethern.
88. f. 177. Dedication of Bradford's Defence of Election. I. 307.
　　　　　　ffaith of Gods election, I meane to beleve.
89. f. 178. Anon. The gracyous comforte of yᵉ holy goste.
90. f. 180. Bradford to Mary Marlar. 2 Feb. 1555. II. 181.
　　f. 180. Bradford's Meditation of the Passion. I. 196.
　　f. 181.　　　,,　　prayer for the presence of God. I. 264.
91. f. 182. Bradford to Royden and Elsing. II. 67.
92. f. 184. Philpot to Lady Vane. VII. 700.
93. f. 186. Bradford. Remarks on a Trial. I. 405.

E. C. C.　　　　　　　　　　　　　　　　　　　　II

94. f. 188. The same to Hopkins. II. 244.
95. f. 190. To the town of Walden. I. 455.
96. f. 193. Bradford. Farewell to his mother. II. 249.
97. f. 194. „ to Philpot. II. 243.
98. f. 195. „ to Rawlins. II. 221. Autogr.
99. f. 197. „ to Aug. Bernher. II. 251. Autogr.
100. f. 198. „ to Lady Vane. II. 142.
101. f. 201. „ to Dr Hill. II. 208.
101*. f. 204. „ to Philpot (=97). II. 243. Autogr.
102. f. 205. „ to Manchester. I. 448. Autogr.
103. f. 207. Fragment of Hullier.
104. f. 208. Petition of Prisoners to the King and Queen. I. 399.
105. f. 209. Bradford. The peace of Christ wch passeth all pleasure.
106. f. 211. Part of the same.
107. f. 212. Th. Lever to Bradford. Zürich. II. 137.
108. f. 213. Careles to Th. Upchare. VIII. 189.
109. f. 215. „ to Aug. Bernher. VIII. 185.
110. f. 217. „ to Tyms etc. VIII. 176.
111. f. 220. Eliz. Longsho to Bradford. II. 226.
112. f. 222. Proclamation of Lady Jane Grey (as Queen).
113. f. 224. Bradford to Coker of Maldon. II. 58.
114. f. 225. Two letters of Hooper.
115. f. 227. Careles? to a woman. As I am ryght sorye.
116. f. 229. „ to Green etc. VIII. 179.
116. f. 231. The same.
117. f. 233. The same.
118. f. 234. The same.
119. f. 236. To Margery C.
120. f. 237. Careles. VIII. 198.
121. f. 238. „ VIII. 192.
122. f. 239. Careles?
123. f. 240. „ to M. C.
124. f. 241. „ VIII. 183.
125. f. 242. „ ? to Bernher, torn.
126. f. 244. „ Albeit frynd Jackson.
127. f. 246. „ to his wife. VIII. 173.
128, 129. f. 247, 249. Declaration of Cranmer against a report "that he shuld set vppe the masse at Canterbury."
130. f. 250. A prayer made by one wch was burned. Foxe VI. 740. Stephen Knight.
131. f. 251. Letter of Hooper printed. The peace and ffavour...I doo muche reioyce.
132. f. 251 b. Th. Matthew to his wife etc. Verses.
Geve yere my childres to my wordes.
133. f. 252 b. Jo. Symson to the congregation in Suffolk etc.
134. f. 254. L. Saunders to his wife. VI. 631.
135. f. 255. Verses. The God that giveth lyfe and light.
136. f. 261. Cranmer (?) to the Queen.
f. 265 b. To Dr Masters and Dr Story.

137. f. 266. Articles against J. Denley. VII. 331 etc.
138. f. 268. ? Bradford. When I consider the state.
139. f. 272. To Bradford. II. 173. Holograph.
140. f. 274. Examination of Ridley and Latimer at Oxford.
141. f. 276. Ridley to Will. Punt. P. S., p. 376.
142. f. 277. Bradford to Mrs Warcup. P. S. II. 185.
143. f. 278. Bernher to Ridley (P. S., p. 381) and Ridley to Bernher. II. 192.
Copy by Bernhere.
144. f. 279. Ridley: Latin notes on the false Decretals. P. S., p. 180.
145. f. 280. Ridley=no. 49. Although Brethren we have of late heard nothynge,
p. 349.
146. f. 281. Ridley, 8 Ap. 1554. I wyshe you grace in God, p. 337.
147. f. 283.=no. 143. (Autograph.)

IV. 1. 18

261.

IV. 2. 29

262.

Probably everything of importance in these volumes has been published by the Parker Society. Only a small proportion of the documents are originals : some of the copies are said to be by Aug. Bernher, and others seem to be by William Tymms. My references to the printed editions are not complete ; I have been unable to identify the anonymous fragments: nor could I have added as many references as I have without the help of a number of slips inserted in IV. 2. 29, by whom I know not.

IV. 3. 31

263.

A collection of printed tracts, $5\frac{1}{8} \times 3\frac{5}{8}$, mostly of early xvith cent., with some additions in manuscript of cent. xvi early.

1. On flyleaves at beginning
   A religious parody of the song " Come over the burn Bessy to me " beginning

Cum ouer the borne bessey my lytyll prety bessey comme
   ouer the borne to me.
The borne hys the world blynde⎫
And bessey is mankynd   ⎬ as she.
So proper cowde I none fynde. ⎭
She daunseth and lepythe
Criste standythe and clepythe
   Come ouer the borne to me.

2. At the end
   Meditationes Bernardi. ff. 18.
   Multi multa sciunt.
3. Stimulus consciencie Bonauenture. ff. 12.
   Ecce descripsi eam tripliciter tibi. Prou. 22. Cum omnis
   sciencia
      —saciamur per christum dominum nostrum. Amen.
   Expl. paruum (?) bonum seu regimine consciencie bonauenture
   quod uocatur fons uite. Ad laudem dei omnip.
4. Speculum monachorum.
   Primo considerare debes. ff. 10.
Seems unfinished.

Yy. 3. 17   C. M. A. 69

264. BIBLIA.

Vellum, 21¾ × 15⅝, ff. 316, double columns of 64 lines. Cent. xv,
in a fine narrow upright English hand, with excellent ornaments of
the time.

On f. 2:

Johannes Newecovrt de Pickwel in Perochia Georgeham in comitatu Deuon. Armiger
dedit istum librum Collegio Emanuelis Cantabrigie. Anno Domini millessimo sex-
centissimo primo etatis dicti Johannis octogessimo
          per me Johannem Newecourt. This is repeated after Apoc.

2 fo. nouerimus.

Collation: 1⁸–26⁸ 27¹² 28⁸ 29⁸ (wants 3) 30⁸–35⁸ 36¹² 37¹² 38⁴ | 39⁶⁷
(4 canc.).

Contents :

Prologues of Jerome. Frater Ambrosius.
               Desiderii mei.
Full border to f. 1 of fine English work, blue, pink, orange, green
   and gold.
Genesis, full border to first page (f. 2 b). On 3 a minutely written
   marginal scholia.

The initials to the books are in gold, usually on a square ground of
half pink, half blue, with patterns in white.

The Prayer of Manasses does not follow 2 Chron.

There is no 3rd Esdras...

Full border to first page of the Psalter, which is Gallican.

Oratio Salomonis follows Ecclus. without a break.

There are stichometric notes to the main divisions of O.T.

After 2 Macc. the Epistle of Eusebius to Carpianus and verses on
the Ten Canons.

Full border to Matt. f. 221.

Proll. to Epistles as in II. 2. 19.

The Epistle to the Laodiceans follows Heb.

Interpretationes nominum in triple columns. Aaz—Zuzim .   . f. 281 *b*

Ending f. 311. Expl. interp. nom. heb. in biblia contentorum
incipientium per diuersas litteras sec. ord. alphabeti. 311 *b* blank.

On 312–316 is a genealogy of Christ in a smaller hand, with
historical notes, chiefly from Methodius, Historia scholastica etc.
with the usual conventional drawings of Babylon, Jerusalem,
the Ark, the Camp etc.

At top

1	2	3	4	5

Lux • firmamentum • mare • terraque • lumina • pisces • Et uolucres •

6

pecudes • fera • reptile cum prothoplasto.

Inc. Considerans historie sacre prolixitatem.

Cain's wife is given as Calmana, Abel's as Delbora.

Noah's is Puarfara, Shem's Parfya, Ham's Cathaflua, Japhet's ffluya.

The genealogy ends with "Christus passus" and list of Apostles.

Text ends

Barnabas in cipro ut patet in legendis eorum.

APPENDIX.

POEM FROM No. 106, f. 11*b*.

Mon queor me dist que doi amer
Mes ieo ne sai ou empler
Amour que tut temps puet durer
Pur ceo su en langour.
Qui mei sauerai enseigner
Ou ficherai mamour.

Si ieo desire biens et richesces
Ieo uei les riches en grant destresces
Au departir doil et tristez
Pur ceo su en languor.
Ieo querai ioie plus adrez
Ou ficherai mamour.

Si ieo desire estre sage
Pruz et bien de haute parage
Ieo uei que tut ceo faut en age
Pur ceo sui en langour.
Ieo queerai ioie en autre age
Ou ficherai mamour.

Si ieo desire mours et uertuez
Pur quei ieo su preise de tutz
Aschun defautz iad desuz
Pur ceo sui en langor.
Ieo querrai ioie pure lasuz
Ou fichera(i) mamour.

Si ieo desire estre honurable
Honur de ceste secle nest que fable
Ffaus et faint et deceiuable
Pur ceo sui en langour.
Ieo querrai ioie plus estable
Ou ficherai mamour.

Ore entendetz dount ieo me affie
Ieo uoiz queraunt oue la marie
Douz ihesu fontaine de uie
Qui garish de langour.
En qui soule ioie est acomplie
La fycherai mamur. Amen.

INDEX.

NOTE. The numbers in heavy type are those of the manuscripts.

Cambridge (*cont.*)
 Scot's Foundation of the University,
  234
 King's College, Register, 97
Cardington, Terrier, 187
Careles, J., Letters, 260. 62 etc. and 262
Cary's Rapture, 68. VI. 12
Catalogue
 of a Library, 188
 of Emman. Coll. MSS., 257
Catechism, a short, 100
Cecill, T., Poem, 68. VI. 6
Chiromancy, tracts, 70. 8, 9
Chronica, 125
 Rolls, 231, 232
 Notes, 246
Chrysostom, Joh. (works in Greek)
 super Matthaeum (Gr.), 12–15
 Serm. de ramis palmarum (Gr.), 59. 2
 Orations, 236. V
 Transl. of relics (Gr.), 236. VI
Chrysostom, J. (works in Latin)
 ad Theodorum, 37. 1
 quod nemo potest laedi, 37. 2
 de compunctione, 67. 3
 (Pseudo-), opus imperfectum, 39, 237
 Sermon (Latin), 56. 5
Clemens Rom.
 Epistle, 65. 5
 on the twelve Fridays, 106. 4
Clerk, Rich., version of S. Mark in Heb., 90
Cockram, Crucifix at, 260. 47
Colet, J., in 1 Cor., 245
Columba, S., 84
Comber, J., 246
Confession
 tracts on, 83, 243. 19
 form of, 229
Cotton, H., p. 129
 J., tracts, 181. VIII
Cranmer, Abp, 260. 4, 136, 262. 51
Cruso, *Euribates*, 185. 3
Curtop, Sermon, 262. 72
Cyprianus (Ps.), duodecim abusiva, 27. 7
Cyrus and Joannes, SS., 236, VI

Daremberg, p. 149
Davenport, H., opinion, 181. III

De negligentia presbyterorum, 27. 18
Denley, J., 260. 137
Devonshire, Earl, discourse, 181. 1
Dictes of Philosophers, 31
Dionysius Periegesis, 32. V
Donne, Dr, Poems, 68. 2
Dorotheus de re occulta, 70. 6
Draycott, letters, 80
Dublin Breviary, 64
Duodecim abusiva seculi, 27. 7
Durandus quaestiones de ordine iurisdict.,
 9. 11
Duthac, S., 84

Earthquakes, notes of, 27. 22
Edmund of Pontigny, S., speculum, 54.
 III, 243. 8
Egidius Romanus de peccato originali,
 243. 17
Egwin, S., 27. 3
England and Wales
 Justices of Peace, 53
 Valor Beneficiorum, 119
English
 Pater noster, etc., 27. 13
 Dictes, 31
 Surgery, 69
 Medicine, 95
 devotion, 72, 246
 poems, 106. 14, 263. 1
 form of confession, 229
 form of excommunication, 248
Ephraem Syrus, S., 236. VI
Epigrams, collection of, 105
Erardis, Gu., Propositio, 9. 14
Ernesti, J. A., 47
Ernulfus, verses on, 38. 6
Eschinden, J., astronomical tracts, 70
Espec, Walter etc. de, 65
Essex, Earl of, 80
 Apology, 181. V
Eunomius, apologeticus, 249
Eusebius (Ps.) de morte Hieronymi,
 252. 1
Excommunication, English form of, 248

Farmer, R., Lectures, 258
Fastolf, John, notes about, 31

CAMBRIDGE: PRINTED BY J. AND C. F. CLAY, AT THE UNIVERSITY PRESS.

For EU product safety concerns, contact us at Calle de José Abascal, 56–1°,
28003 Madrid, Spain or eugpsr@cambridge.org.

 www.ingramcontent.com/pod-product-compliance
Ingram Content Group UK Ltd.
Pitfield, Milton Keynes, MK11 3LW, UK
UKHW012345130625
459647UK00009B/532